D0353573

Made in Britain

Books that make you better

Books that make you better. That make you *be* better, *do* better, *feel* better. Whether you want to upgrade your personal skills or change your job, whether you want to improve your managerial style, become a more powerful communicator, or be stimulated and inspired as you work.

Prentice Hall Business is leading the field with a new breed of skills, careers and development books. Books that are a cut above the mainstream – in topic, content and delivery – with an edge and verve that will make you better, with less effort.

Books that are as sharp and smart as you are.

Prentice Hall Business.
We work harder – so you don't have to.

For more details on products, and to contact us, visit
www.pearsoned.co.uk

Steven D'Souza
Patrick Clarke

MADE IN BRITAIN

Inspirational role models from British Black and Minority Ethnic communities

Harlow, England • London • New York • Boston • San Francisco • Toronto • Sydney • Singapore • Hong Kong
Tokyo • Seoul • Taipei • New Delhi • Cape Town • Madrid • Mexico City • Amsterdam • Munich • Paris • Milan

PEARSON EDUCATION LIMITED

Edinburgh Gate
Harlow CM20 2JE
Tel: +44 (0)1279 623623
Fax: +44 (0)1279 431059
Website: www.pearsoned.co.uk

301·451

First published in Great Britain in 2005

© Steven D'Souza and Patrick Clarke 2005

The rights of Steven D'Souza and Patrick Clarke to be identified as authors of this work have been asserted by them in accordance with the Copyright, Designs and Patents Act 1988.

ISBN-10: 0 273 70600 4
ISBN-13: 978 0 273 70600 7

British Library Cataloguing-in-Publication Data
A catalogue record for this book is available from the British Library

Library of Congress Cataloging-in-Publication Data
D'Souza, Steven.
Made in Britain : inspirational role models from British Black and Minority Ethnic communities / Steven D'Souza
p. cm
ISBN 0–273–706000–4 (alk. paper)
1. Minorities—Great Britain—Interviews. 2. Role Models—Great Britain—Biography. I. Title

DA125.A1D67 2005
305.5'6'092241—dc22
[B] 2005048906

All rights reserved. No part of this publication may be reproduced, stored in a retrieval system, or transmitted in any form or by any means, electronic, mechanical, photocopying, recording or otherwise, without either the prior written permission of the publisher or a licence permitting restricted copying in the United Kingdom issued by the Copyright Licensing Agency Ltd, 90 Tottenham Court Road, London W1T 4LP. This book may not be lent, resold, hired out or otherwise disposed of by way of trade in any form of binding or cover other than that in which it is published, without the prior consent of the Publishers.

10 9 8 7 6 5 4 3 2
09 08 07 06 05

'If' by Rudyard Kipling is reproduced with permission of A P Watt Ltd on behalf of The National Trust for Places of Historic Interest or Natural Beauty

Typeset in 11pt Minion by 70
Printed and bound by Bell & Bain Ltd, Glasgow

The Publisher's policy is to use paper manufactured from sustainable forests.

Contents

Foreword vii

Introduction 1

Never give up 33
Partha Dey

Bringing the 'gift of life' to life 45
Beverley De Gale and Orin Lewis

Dressed for success 55
Asif Kisson

To be Bond or not to be Bond 65
Colin Salmon

Everything is negotiable 75
Bill Morris

A Lady among Lords 83
Baroness Uddin

Grand Canyons 93
Karan Bilimoria

Networking up 105
Saundra Glenn

The heart and soul of politics 115
Ram Gidoomal CBE

Living out loud 127
Angie Le Mar

The 1% Club 139
Janet Soo-Chung

The sky's the limit 149
Mohan Ahad

Keeping London safe 157
Tarique Ghaffur

No ivory towers 165
David Adjaye

How do we learn from role models? 175

Appendix 201

'There is no black in the Union Jack' 203

Resources 217

Publisher's acknowledgements 234

Authors' acknowledgements 235

About the authors 237

Foreword

Gary Phillips, headteacher at Lilian Baylis Technology School, Lambeth

Young people talk about their aspirations and the aspirations that their family, friends and community have for them. They also talk about what they believe society in general expects of them and how the media shapes their views and the views of others.

The aspirations that young people have for themselves need to be nurtured and challenged. In some cases aspirations can be empowering and motivating whilst in other cases they can lead to low self esteem and a feeling of hopelessness.

Role models play a vital role in supporting the aspirations of young people. They show young people that they can achieve whatever they want to achieve. Through their everyday work as well as through their media profile and biographies, role models demonstrate how to take the steps required to achieve. This leads to the aspirations of young people being nurtured and realised.

Black and Minority Ethnic (BME) young people, like all young people, need role models from every area of society but in particular role models from a BME background. This is due to the under-representation of appropriate BME role models in the media and other professions. This under-representation sends a clear message to some young people. Some interpret it as being due to a lack of recognition of the achievements of BME people whilst others interpret it as it being harder for

BME people to succeed in some professions. Whatever the explanation, and it is probably a combination of both, this under-representation does not support the aspirations of young people.

This book attempts to address these issues. It details, through the use of interviews, the journeys that a selection of BME achievers have made. Many have had to overcome significant barriers whilst others have had to come to terms with personal issues. However all have achieved success through hard work, determination and the ability to learn from others.

Many of the people interviewed for this book may be new to you. If they are I hope you will ask yourself why this is. More importantly I hope you will, as the authors have done, commit to ensuring that this continued lack of recognition is addressed. This is vital if we are to collectively address the issues raised in the excellent final chapter 'There is no black in the Union Jack'.

This book is not only required reading for young people, but for all of us who seek positive change in our schools and society.

Introduction

This book is written with one aim: to inspire you to reach for your dreams and discover your purpose.

We hope it will convince you that you are a valuable part of British society and have great potential that, when realised, will benefit not only you but many others too. This applies whether you are young or older, and whether you are a student, manager, housewife or chief executive!

The inspiration in this book comes in the form of real people – people who have achieved something special in their lives and careers, sometimes against the odds, but people like you and me all the same. We are all touched by the examples of others, positively or negatively. As children, our early influences come from parents, friends and teachers and then increasingly from TV, the mass media and the wider world. The influence of role models is powerful. It was a positive role model who changed the life of Helen Keller, who was born blind, deaf and unable to speak, and inspired her to learn to read, write and teach. Negative role models have led others to turn to gun crime or drugs in order to be like their anti-heroes. Some role models are high profile, while others are the ordinary heroes, people who have quietly achieved so much.

The focus of the book is role models and inspiring people from British Black and Minority Ethnic (BME) communities. The role models we've chosen are deliberately diverse: they include a rocket scientist, a hat maker, the founder of a beer company, a former general secretary of a trade union, an award-winning architect, an NHS chief executive and one couple whose role model is their son. Yet what's surprising is how much they have in common. We investigate what they can teach us about being successful – on their terms. The stories, inspiration and ideas can benefit anyone, regardless of background.

This book is intended to help you consciously use role models as a powerful force in your life to achieve your dreams. Ultimately we hope it will also help you recognise that you too can be a role model, with the ability to influence the potential of others. Success doesn't come from imitating others but through finding and expressing your own 'voice' and sharing your unique gifts with others.

We don't know why you are reading this book – though it would be really interesting to know. Perhaps you saw it in your library. Possibly you were bought a copy. Maybe your friend is reading it and you grabbed it from them to look at the photos. Whatever the reason, and whether you call yourself black, white, neither, or any shade in between, we are confident you will find something here that is valuable. This book is written for you.

How were the role models in the book selected?

The choice of role models in this book is entirely personal and our responsibility. Some of the people are public figures, others aren't. We chose each of them because we felt we could learn something from their life experience and thought they had something valuable to share with other people. In short, they inspired us. They were willing to share themselves, warts and all, and tell us how they got to where they are now. All of the interviewees are British BMEs – if they weren't born in Britain, they have spent a large part of their lives in the UK.

The interviews are not CVs – they aim to be deeper. They look at questions such as: How do they define success? Has their cultural identity influenced them? What gives them inspiration? What lessons have they learned as they have progressed in their field? What disappointments or failures did they have and how did they respond? Would they do anything different if they could choose again? And lastly, what advice would they impart?

If you don't agree with our selection of role models, that's fine. The whole idea of role models is that you choose your own. We can't tell you who yours should be – we can only offer you an insight into people who are role models to others, in the hope they will inspire you too. Perhaps you might think of who you would have chosen and this will spur you to make your own list, as others have.

What is important is what we can learn from them and, more importantly, what can we take away about ourselves. We look more at how to learn from role models (even those who are no longer with us) on page 173.

Why a book on BME role models?

> *'We don't see why black people would need role models. The book just wouldn't work.'*
>
> An unnamed publishing company, July 2004

> *'We would love to publish this book . . . this is a really important and exciting project.'*
>
> Pearson, February 2005

Between the two statements above a miracle occurred. Besides finding a publisher who believed in this project (thank you,

Rachael!), 6,000 copies of this book were sold before Patrick and I had finished it. It happened for one reason. The book's message was considered important enough for people to give it their full support. If the publishers were amazed, we were more so.

I (Steven) have a confession. If you had spoken to me a little under ten years ago and told me that I would write a book on role models drawn from British Black and Minority Ethnic communities, I would have looked at you with cynical compassion. Actually, if you had told me that I would write a book on anything, you wouldn't have heard anything over the laughter.

In order to understand why I did want to spend part of my life writing this book rather than enjoying the evening with friends, doing nothing, lazing in a bubble bath or dancing the night away, I would like to share with you a very small part of my own life story. I have found I remember stories better than facts and one of the best ways to get to know anyone is to listen to what they have experienced.

Like the majority of black and minority ethnic people in the UK today, I was born here. I consider myself British and also Goan. Goa is a state in South India where my parents lived before they came to the UK. It's popularly known as the place where all the hippies went to chill out on the beaches in the 60s and where my friends headed after university for full moon parties and the latest trance tunes.

I could write pages and pages on why I chose the label 'British' rather than 'English' but at this point let me say that I cannot define myself as English because I feel the majority of people would never accept me as English. I shall say more on self-definition in a little while.

I am British – my passport says so, the fact that I was born here says so (it was before the Nationality Act of 1981), but the important fact that I find spicy food too hot is the real evidence, according to my parents! However, I am also Goan because we have a unique culture, language and identity as a community, a lot of which is based happily around food.

I remember seeing a book recently entitled *All I really need to know I learned in kindergarten.* I know I certainly learned more outside of school than in it. Between the daily lumpy custard and the impossible task of having to stand perfectly still when the whistle blew, I liked going to school, but mostly to be with friends. Educational play interrupted by lessons. It's where I learned that if I didn't support Liverpool I would get a punch on the arm and the next term if I didn't support Arsenal it was still the same. On the playground, in the sand pit, we were all just children. Equally noisy and probably equally frustrating to the teachers.

I grew up on a predominately white, working-class council estate. Idyllic really. This was my real classroom. My brother and I would play football with friends till the sun went down and then we would all play more, long after the ball had been swallowed by twilight or fallen into the school caretaker's garden. In between the joy of football we had all the other adventures of youth.

But not all days were like this. Some days were different. 'Why did they put a firework through our letter box?', I remember asking my mum, wondering what would have happened if one of us had gone to answer the door. 'Why are they throwing stones at our window?', I remember thinking as I tried to peer from behind the net curtains to see but not be seen, hoping the window wouldn't break when a stone or half-brick was thrown at it.

I got the answer to 'Why?' when I was nine. It was a hot sunny July day and I was sitting on my porch with one of my best friends from school, flicking through a free catalogue and wondering which trainers to buy – Nike or Puma. Just looking at the trainers was the fun part. Even if we didn't have the pocket money, our imaginations ran wild.

The afternoon was drawing on and we had been at my house all day. I was getting bored. Very bored. I suggested that we went to play at my friend's house. 'It's fine with me,' he replied, 'but we can't.'

'Why?' I asked.

'Well, it's nothing to do with me,' he replied, genuinely apologetic, 'but my older brother doesn't like black people. I'm sorry but you can't come or he'll beat you up.'

I changed the subject but his response changed me. Why had he called me 'black'? I didn't understand. 'I'm not 'black', I'm Indian, Goan. My skin is brown,' I thought to myself, dismissing his stupidity and obvious colour-blindness. I also thought, 'Is his brother crazy?' We continued playing at mine. I reflect now and wonder why I didn't challenge him further. Had he always known that his friend was 'black'? Why did I not know earlier? Why did I not 'feel' different?

As I grew older the stones took on a direction. I would walk to middle school each day and be greeted by 'Paki', this from my best friend. Walking to the shops I would be called 'black bastard', trying not to get run over by teenagers on motorcycles as I went. Aged about ten years old in Dunstable, a predominately white town, I was asked politely by some adults why I was not in Bury Park, an area of Luton with a high minority ethnic population. I told my parents nothing of this. I wondered whether it was just me who was affected by this. Until that point I thought that perhaps it was only children who were cruel to other children. It took me a long while to understand, and an even longer time to accept, that adults could share the same views. I slowly became aware that although I could define myself, it was others who defined me, by my skin colour. I could be Goan, Indian and British even, but I was still a 'Paki' because I looked different.

That summer I began to distinguish 'NF', the symbol of the National Front, from what I initially thought was 'WF', which at the time was the Wrestling Federation and very popular at school. Soon enough I noticed this symbol everywhere, painted on walls, scratched on bus stops and near stickers plastered in phone boxes, saying, 'Attack Zionist Imperialism'. 'Why are English people concerned with Jewish politics?' I wondered. NF was once painted in white on the side of our house. Were we political?

Growing up, incidents of racism were sporadic and I hoped that as I got older I would leave discrimination behind. I thought that if I ignored it the problems would go away. My parents, to protect us, rarely seemed to talk about it, except on the occasions when things happened that you couldn't ignore. Then they would say, 'It's not that bad . . . don't make a big deal, it's just kids'. I walked to the shops with my mum once and two people on a bike kept saying, 'put, put, ding, ding' and kicking her shopping trolley. We called the police that afternoon, but like so many other times nothing came of it. (If you are a victim of racism in public today, there is a specific criminal offence to protect you from harassment. The last thing to do is to ignore it.)

Moving away from home and going to university in the leafy London borough of Richmond was my way out. To pretend that I was not different, that racism doesn't happen, will not happen. Maybe eventually I would forget and even come to believe that it didn't happen. 'Why do black people need role models?' And 'What do you mean by black anyway?' These weren't the questions of somebody who hadn't experienced racism or had never desperately wanted to see representation of people from similar backgrounds. These were my questions.

My attitude changed the day when, whilst working at a play scheme, an African girl, Brigitte Bakodie, gave me a leaflet. It was for a leadership programme for 'Black and Minority Ethnic' undergraduates to develop them as leaders. 'How racist,' I thought. 'Why do these people need special treatment? What do they mean by calling themselves "black and minority ethnic" anyway? They should just get on with life just like everyone else. Just like me.' The idea that difference could be accepted was alien to me.

The programme, called the Windsor Fellowship, offered work placements, sponsorship from leading UK companies and fantastic development seminars. 'Perhaps I should check this out,' I thought. 'Sponsorship could definitely help with student loans and the extra drink at the bar even if I have to pretend to be "black".'

I got on the programme, but Brigitte didn't and I never saw her again. (If you are reading this – thank you.)

There was no money. Instead every term I joined a group of other students who were also 'black and minority ethnic' while we worked long weekends developing skills such as presenting, working in teams and managing ourselves and others. Many of the students had career aspirations to join companies that I had not even heard of. Some were clearly over-achievers and needed 'chill-out' time. I wondered, 'Why do they have to try so hard?' Later I learned. If you keep reading, you will too.

Seminar after seminar each of the students began to inspire me in some way. Whether to be an investment banker, a legal eagle or an IT whizz kid, all of these students wanted to be leaders in their communities and to make a difference to others. They wanted to achieve success – but without sacrificing their culture or forgetting the communities they had come from. Many of them, like me, were the first people in their immediate families to go on to university. For some of them English was not the mother tongue, not at home.

Speaking with other 'Fellows', as we were called, we began to share our stories. We learned to look at our identity and culture not as something to be ashamed of or to move away from but rather as something which we could own, accept and even celebrate.

For the first time in my life I was beginning to accept that I was different, that in the world's eyes I was 'black' and I was beginning to notice that I didn't want to ignore or hide from that.

If at nine I had learned 'why' I was being treated differently, it took me until the age of 21 to accept and learn 'what' being treated differently would mean not only for me but for all those like me who are visibly different in Britain today.

Let's look at another story now. Patrick is my co-author and his experience is one of being brought up in Jamaica and coming to Britain as a child. Patrick is often asked to be a mentor and is a role model to many people, within his company and his community. When you read his story it is obvious why. Patrick's account shows how a good role model at a vital time had a huge influence on his life and how his experiences make him a great role model for others.

Keeping the lights on – Patrick's story

When I tell people about my life they always seem to be inspired by it. To me it is not that special because it is my life and I have become accustomed to it.

Having lived in the UK for many years, I am used to people's reaction when I say I was born in Jamaica. They tend to imagine sun, sand, sea and idyllic beaches. While for some that might be their experience of Jamaica, for me and many others it could not be further from the truth. In reality whilst I now know that life was poor and basic when compared with life now, if I had a choice then I would much rather be poor and have a basic life in Jamaica than in the UK.

Home in Jamaica was the back half of a building which included two rooms, each the size of a small to medium-sized garden shed, and a shop. In the Caribbean it was not unusual

The real Jamaica – Patrick's childhood home

Windsurfers on Negril beach, Jamaica

for children to be raised by grandparents or aunties, and I was raised by my great-aunt. It was only after I returned to Jamaica in the mid 1980s that I realised I had lived in no mansion.

I left Jamaica for England at the age of eight. When I returned I was 23 and working as an electrical engineer. My colleagues were envious of me having family in the Caribbean and being able to spend so much time there at little cost. The challenge in my mind was whether I should tell them that although Jamaica is beautiful, I was not accustomed to the sort of lifestyle portrayed in glossy travel brochures. In time I realised that there was no point giving people false impressions. I am proud of my background and felt I should not be concerned about what other people would think. After all, this is one of the many bricks in the building of Patrick Clarke.

Patrick's outside toilet

Telling it like it is

For many years I have made presentations to schoolchildren during morning assemblies or on special school occasions. I am usually invited under the banner 'Role Model'. In 2004 I gave a presentation to a school in Clapham, South London, which remains in my mind for two reasons. The children, aged 11 to

Inside Patrick's home in Jamaica

16 and from diverse backgrounds, knew that my role at work at the time was, in simple terms, to 'keep the lights on in London'. The aim of my interactive presentation was to take them on a journey from the beginning of my life to where I was at the time. The children saw a picture of the two-roomed house and many other aspects of my life. When I showed the class the picture of my house, I asked them what they believed the building was used for. Some said it was a shed, others said a toilet, but one Ugandan boy said, 'It's your house, sir; it is like some of our houses in Africa.' The boy, who had been in the country for only about five years, was able to identify with much of my life because it was so similar to his own life in Africa. The building blocks in my life related to his building blocks. He then just needed to see all my remaining building blocks and how they linked up in order to see what was possible for him.

Patrick (left) and his older brother

It is very important for positive role models to create the opportunity for others to link into aspects of their development and to see how their lives progressed from there.

The Ugandan boy also realised from my presentation that it was OK to talk about your past, even if it doesn't apparently have the same standards as the people around you.

After this presentation an Australian girl came up to me and said she could identify with some of my early school experiences in the UK. When she arrived at her new school the class expected her to be sitting in a corner drinking Foster's lager. She too was able to link into early aspects of my life in the UK and how people can stereotype you. This opened my mind to fully realising that role modelling is not only about race or colour.

My early years

There were only two rooms in my house; the bathroom was effectively the adjacent river flowing fast from the local foothills near to the blue mountain range (where the famous coffee is grown). It was pure, clean and very warm. We used it for all our water needs: cooking, drinking, washing clothing, bathing and playing. We would also catch fresh-water prawns and eels and eat them that same day. Sadly, this fast-flowing river is now only a trickle.

Our kitchen was situated directly outside the main entrance to the house; it was simply a large pile of rock between which we would ignite a fire using wood or coal. We used this method to cook some of the tastiest Caribbean dishes. Alas, this generation of UK-born Jamaicans simply cannot replicate this quality, even when using modern high-tech kitchens.

The house was constructed with a zinc roof, which would leak during the heavy Caribbean rainfall. More importantly, if you have never slept under a zinc roof while it's raining, you should try it. It is the most wonderful and therapeutic feeling, lying in bed hearing that sound. The two rooms were each large enough to fit a small bed – smaller than a double but larger than a single – and my great-aunt, brother and I would sleep comfortably in this bed.

We would play in the road during the evenings and weekends (passing vehicles were rare) and at night the moonshine would make up for the lack of electricity, lighting up our play, just like those old black-and-white films. We would chat all night and tell stories.

School in Jamaica was tough. Within spitting distance of my house, every child in the valley attended this school, except the few whose parents had money to send them to school in the capital, Kingston. Typically four classes were taught in the same room, about the size of a small church hall. My greatest memory of school is using slate and chalks for the equivalent of an exercise book and pen. We would use the chalk to write on the slate, then when one side was full we would turn it over and continue writing on the other side and when that side was full we would turn it over and rub out what was just written and continue to write new text. It was what I was accustomed to so it seemed normal. I know you are probably wondering how we ever learned anything but we did.

At the time in Jamaica children learned to respect each other and especially their elders. My great-aunt always expected a good work ethic and results telling me that manners maketh a man and that manners would take me through this world. She taught me to respect people at all times and to be honest and act with integrity. This was very much aligned to the strong Christian values which were expected from me and most children growing up in Jamaica. These values remained with me and were strengthened when I became a born-again Christian in the late 70s. Regrettably, and to my detriment, I have not remained as committed to the faith as I once was.

A new life

When I arrived in the UK with my older brother it was a cold February day. I was met by my mother and father, people I really didn't know; they could have been anyone. I also met my cheeky little brother and I can still hear him asking, 'Who are those two boys?' When my mother told him, 'They are your brothers', he responded, 'No, they can't be, they are too black.' My younger brother had lived in this country all his life and was of a lighter complexion; all of a sudden he was confronted by these two dark-skinned boys who were supposed to be his older brothers.

We drove from Heathrow Airport to my new home in Brixton, South London. It had some similarity to my home in Jamaica. It was a large three-storey Victorian house in Dalyell Road but my parents could afford to rent only two rooms, one bedroom and a living room. At nights the settee would convert to a bed and all three boys would sleep in it pretending not to watch the TV which was in the same room. Our parents soon wised up to this so we had to sleep with the sheets over our heads. So from two rooms in Jamaica to two cold rooms in Brixton. We shared a bathroom and a kitchen with four other families from Jamaica. In all about 20 people lived in this house. Yet apart from the cold, to me it was luxury.

There were some simple aspects of life which caused great difficulty. I could not accept these two people as my parents. My younger brother did not accept us as his brothers. I spoke with a strong Jamaican accent, as you would expect. My parents, who had been living in the country for over eight years, did not like the way I spoke and would consistently tell me to speak properly. I did not understand how else they expected me to speak; as far as I was concerned my language was fine. In fact, I had great difficulty understanding the so-called 'Queen's English'.

There was more. Imagine, for instance, seeing and eating baked beans for the first time. In the first 24 hours I did not recognise most things I was given to eat, let alone knew whether I liked them. My younger brother was in the background eating away and continued to feel we were unusual, especially after we refused to eat this unusual food. It took almost a decade before

I really began to feel comfortable with my new-found family.

My mother used to tell me that I would never amount to anything; she always told us that the other children in the area were better than us. I have heard many famous and successful people recount having the same said to them, usually by a teacher. Nick Faldo was told by his teacher that he would never achieve in life, and look at him now. Just tell me I can't do something, set me that challenge and I will prove you wrong. Always believe in yourself.

The school years

The next major phase in my life in the UK came when I went to school, a primary school in Brixton called Santley School, now the site of luxury flats. Again, imagine this skinny little boy just arrived from sunny Jamaica, walking to school (about three-quarters of a mile) in freezing conditions, wearing grey shorts with long socks, a hand-knitted cardigan, coat, balaclava and gloves. I did not understand what was happening to my body, I was so cold and numb. School life was difficult enough without the pain caused by the effects of the cold. The other children saw me as different and strange, I spoke funny and they did not understand me. As children do, they persecuted me mercilessly. My teacher lost patience with me – I was too cold to get involved with the lessons, my lips were numb so I could not speak clearly and my fingers were still frozen so I could not hold the pencil.

Something had to give. After a few weeks of this new country and school my pent-up frustration boiled over in anger and violent behaviour. I resorted to throwing chairs (those little chairs that I now sit on at parents' evening) across the room when it all became too much, my way of saying I needed help. If my parents had known it would not have been worth going home those evenings: West Indian parents were disciplinarians and did not tolerate this type of behaviour. Those were difficult days; there was no refuge either at home or at school.

When I look back it seems life was in shades of grey – there was no colour, no laughter, no fun at home. I was still adjusting. When I think about those days I remember the smelly and dangerous paraffin heaters we needed to keep the house warm. After the wick of the paraffin heater was turned down, the winter nights were bitter. It was even worse in the mornings, waking up in a cold house and then having to use a cold bathroom. I just wanted to go back home to Jamaica.

I am not proud of my behaviour in my early school years and would not recommend it to any young person growing up today. But even in those circumstances I was a role model (negative) to other young boys, especially those who had recently arrived from the Caribbean and were facing the same difficulties. When I think back to this past I am not ashamed of my actions; rather, it helps me to better understand why I am the way I am today.

Someone to show me the way

I really needed a role model in my life at that time and fortunately my uncle was not far away. He was and still is the biggest role model in my life. He had come to the UK some years before me and worked for the GPO and then the Post Office after it separated from the telecoms side (BT).

Every Friday night my brothers and I would go to his house where he would give us extra tuition in maths and English. He gave up his Friday nights to spend time with us. Like me, my uncle never studied full time – evening classes were the only real option open to him. After many years of studying at various levels he eventually achieved an MA in Economics. I thought, what a wonderful achievement, he must be brainy because in my eyes anyone who had a degree was brainy. No one in our family had ever achieved such dizzy heights. So I was very proud of him and wanted to follow in his footsteps.

My uncle has always encouraged me. His tactic was to motivate me by telling me that I would never be as good as him. It worked – just tell me I can't do or achieve something and I will go out of my way to prove you wrong. My uncle is now working with the Jamaican government (a civil servant) and occasionally writes speeches for P.J. Patterson, the Prime Minister, and posts them to me to read. But I know he is showing off and is really using this as a tactic to make sure I aim higher and always try to do better than him. I never understood why he bothered to spend so much time with us when he could have spent his time relaxing or doing something more interesting.

After studying at three primary schools it was time for me to start secondary school. In those days most children went to the local comprehensive unless they met the criteria in which case they might attend the grammar school instead. My secondary school was Kennington Boys' School, now a girls' school. Over 2,000 children attended this school on two sites. A school this size was quite typical in the 70s. Due to my very poor early years, my first class at Kennington School was for children with learning difficulties. Fortunately, however, as I went through school I had the continued support and guidance of my uncle, who remained my role model. There was no way I could let him down. As I progressed through what was a very poor school (in today's terminology it would be called a failing school), I began to realise that I needed to get out of this mess. Like many young black men, sports and music were what attracted me most. I was a very good sportsman, especially when it came to football, and spent every spare moment kicking a ball. I played for the school on a number of occasions and won the school five-a-side tournament every year. This was a real success since I had not even understood the rules when I arrived in the UK a few years earlier. I would pick up the ball and run to the goalkeeper with it. Imagine the frustration of the other children!

Making the grade

The teachers in this new school did not really understand me or any of the children who had recently arrived from the Caribbean. Some would set us a task at the start of the lesson, leave us and return at the end. Surprisingly, no work got done while the teacher was away – we loved the freedom and spent most of the time playing games such as dominoes and cards. It did not matter to us that we were not receiving any teaching and the teachers did not care much.

There was no real order in the school and so it was that at 15 I sat six CSEs and achieved three grade 2s and three grade 3s – useless qualifications. My uncle was disappointed, although my parents did not really understand the grading system so 2s and 3s sounded OK to them. This woke me up – I began to realise that I would get nowhere in school or life unless I put my head down and tried harder.

A new role

I was now sixteen and about to start my last year in the sixth form when, to my surprise, the headmaster asked me to be head boy for that year (they were really scraping the barrel). I accepted and realised that I had to set an example for younger boys in the school. I was now a role model in my own right – younger boys were looking up to me. I started to buckle down. I kept thinking about the 3 million people unemployed in the late 70s and the difficulties I would have getting a job. While most teachers in the school were lazy and didn't bother with us, the school was lucky to attract a young white maths teacher who took a keen interest. He gave eight of us extra maths sessions in his own time after school twice a week. Every one of us in these after-school sessions achieved either grade A or B later that year. These were children who prior to this could not even achieve a CSE grade 1. I eventually passed four other O-levels that year, all at Grade A, B or C. This single event made me realise that my school had failed me miserably. It took a teacher who really cared to give us self-belief – he always told us that we could do it, he believed in us. I still believe that this was the turning point in my life – it was as if my eyes were opened to how badly my school and teachers had failed me.

I was now a role model to the younger boys – they had not been accustomed to many black boys passing CSEs, let alone achieving five O-levels (including one in the difficult subject of maths). I had this new-found feeling of responsibility and I was proud of my achievements. Six years earlier I started in a class for children with learning difficulties. Ten years earlier I had just arrived in the country and was trying to adjust to different primary schools, my new-found family and the climate. When people tell me I have done well, I always wonder how much better I could have done had I had a better education. Leaving a failing school with five O-levels was a great achievement, but I left feeling bitter because of the injustice I had suffered for the past six years. As I write these words I would just like to say thank you to Mr Turner, my maths teacher – you gave me more than just an O-level in maths, you helped me to realise that I have great potential and with the correct application can do great things.

Starting work

Life became a lot more serious for me, facing the possibility of leaving school with no work, like 3 million other people. My father's advice was to learn a trade – plumbing, carpentry, etc – his view was that so long as I had a skill no one could take it away from me and I would have plenty of opportunities to get work. He wanted me to work with BT as he did, repairing telephone circuits, but my interest lay in electricity. I was always breaking open TVs and radios to see what was inside. (In fact, my first real ambition was to be a pilot, so I applied to British

Airways for an interview, but not surprisingly to me, I was unsuccessful.) I applied to many engineering companies, including BT, but was unsuccessful with most. London Electricity was the first company to call me for an aptitude test and interview. I passed the aptitude test with flying colours, but to my disappointment I was told that I did so well they would be wasting my time accepting me onto the apprenticeship programme. They said I would be bored in no time, I would find being an electrician too easy. To my surprise they recommended that I apply for one of the roles as a trainee engineer. I thought I would be wasting my time since I would be in competition with boys who had had a better level of education. But at the interview for this bigger role I impressed them with my life story and how I had got to this point in my life ten years after coming to the UK. I believe they saw a lot of grit and character and I am sure that is what tilted the offer of a job in my favour. Always believe in yourself, warts and all, but before you can believe in yourself you must know who you are.

When you look back at it, the odds were stacked against me, yet six years later, here I was with a good job, working for a large utility company.

I still did not believe it. Was I really going to make it through this four-year training programme? Surely all the other new trainees were better than me? Some started with A-levels and were placed on the training programme which led to a degree in Electrical Engineering. I started with O-levels and was placed with about seven other boys on the Technician Engineers training course, which after four years eventually led to an HNC (Higher National Certificate) in Electrical Engineering. Interestingly, from a career perspective I have progressed further than all my then better qualified colleagues, some of whom still work for the same company.

Climbing the career ladder

After four years of academic training it was time to start getting my career on track, but how far did I want to go? Bearing in mind I had never expected to be at this level in a company like this, I was happy with simply reaching this basic stage. The early years in the company had uncanny similarities to starting at a new school. It was and still is a great company to work for, but role models, people who I could identify with and who I believed cared about me, were missing. That was when I realised that a role model does not have to be the same colour as me. There were a couple of white senior managers in the company who really cared about developing people, especially those who were interested in their personal development. I suppose they were not really role models, more mentors, people who helped me with direction and gave me the confidence to believe that I could achieve more than the relatively low targets I had set myself. These people did not know that they were my mentors or role models. They did what they did because they could see the ability in me which could be used for their own career gains.

From there to here

Through hard work and support from key people throughout my career I have made it to very near the top of the company I currently work for. I am now Director of Human Resources and Communications for a branch of EDF Energy, employing nearly 4,000 people. During the most recent branch reorganisation my direct boss asked me to step up to a more senior role, doing something totally different to my previous role – from engineering to HR. For me this demonstrates real confidence from my boss and the executive of the company; after all, it is a risk as I am totally untried and tested in this arena.

As I have risen through the ranks of the organisation, it has always been important to me to keep my feet on the ground and stay in touch with people at all levels. I still get the reaction from some people, 'How did he get there?' Pleasingly, many of those in the organisation to whom I am a natural role model called after my appointment to say how proud they were of me. This gives me a great lift and reminds me that as well as my HR and communications responsibility, I have a responsibility to the people who look up to me for example, motivation, inspiration and direction.

In this role and in my previous senior roles I have practised being an active mentor and role model to many. I am particularly proud of the mentoring and role-model relationship I have had with a young man called Marco Coltelli. He has risen from a 14-year-old work placement student to one of the branch's most senior customer services manager 12 years later. A female member of staff famously said to Marc, 'I was speaking to your dad today.' Marc did not really understand since there was no way this lady could have met his dad. She then went on to say she was confused since Patrick was black and Marco was white, so how could I be his dad? Of course she was joking! She explained that she met me and after a lengthy conversation realised that the relationship was like a father to a son. In fact, what she was seeing was a strong, longstanding mentor/mentee relationship that worked. From time to time other employees would say to Marc, 'You are just like Patrick Clarke.' In life people often try to emulate aspects of their role models or mentors, as I have done with my uncle.

As a role model to many of the BME employees within the company I always try to stay close and in touch with them, including regular communications and informal networks. This is my attempt to help them understand better who I am and to ensure they feel comfortable in engaging with me about any issues, in particular helping them to understand how I made it to this senior level. It is all about helping them to see the building blocks. For many years I have literally used a building blocks model to set targets for my career. I draw a brick wall four bricks high and about four bricks wide. Each brick is a personal objective for the future – some are work related and others are in my private life. It is important to get the balance. As I achieve them I colour in the bricks until every brick is filled in. The four foundation bricks have objectives which must be achieved before any of the other bricks can be filled in.

I recently attended a European company-wide conference where over 1,000 senior managers from all over the world were present. I was one of only two black managers at this conference. People know me because in most work environments I stand out. The more junior black employees ask me how I cope with this. I tell them it is not a problem, I am confident about who I am and have clearly demonstrated my skills and abilities at every level.

Incidentally, 20 years after being placed in a class for children with learning difficulties, I achieved an MBA with distinction and various other high-level qualifications. I have received three company awards during the past 11 years, one of which was based on the votes of my fellow senior managers. Some of my more junior BME colleagues often ask me why they are not finding it as easy to break through what is sometimes perceived as a glass ceiling. I can't provide answers for their situations, but I am able to explain how I do it and the ammunition I believe is required to break that glass, such as education, experience, skills, attitude, etc.

Prior to my recent appointment as Director of HR and Communications, I held day-to-day responsibility for keeping the electricity flowing in London – as I would say, 'keeping the lights on', a role which I was immensely proud to do. As Head of the Networks for London I would often visit senior people in large blue-chip companies. When I first stepped into their offices you could see those thought bubbles saying, 'is this really Patrick Clarke?' Understandably they did not expect to see a black man in charge of keeping the lights on in London. On other occasions I would visit with some of my more junior white colleagues and the customer automatically assumed they were my boss.

Prior to this exciting role I was General Manager of a subsidiary company within the same group of companies, with a turnover of £60 million a year, employing over 500 people plus contractors. Even this I would never have believed when I was placed in that class, labelled with learning difficulties, in a failing school.

In my past and current roles I have really felt the weight of being a role model. Many BME employees look up to me and feel proud; their own confidence and esteem have risen because of where I sit in the company. They feel that my elevation within the organisation is not only a statement about me, it is also a positive statement about them as a collection or community of people. My parents and uncle back in the Caribbean are immensely proud of me. My friends talk about me and refer to me as their standard bearer.

My wife Sonji was born in this country of Caribbean parents (I call her English and I am definitely Jamaican) and has recently reached the heady height of Consultant Obstetrician and Gynaecologist. So when our children go to school they say their mother is a doctor and their father turns on the lights in London. I think I need to do some more work to help my children better understand what my role entails! When I was appointed to my current role, my ten-year-old son asked me whether the job involved fixing telephones. He understood communications as relating to telephones and thought I had changed from electricity to telecoms. Clearly there is much work to be done here before my three little boys see me as their role model.

Playing a role in the community

Every month that passed saw a more mature Patrick, keen to make the most of his future and learn from some of the mistakes and shortcomings in earlier life. I decided that I needed to help others coming into and through the school system. In my late teens and early 20s, when many of my friends and peers were spending much of their time having fun in bars, clubs or other places of entertainment, I started getting involved with a variety of community activities. Just four years after leaving school I became a governor at a local school. I could still see many of the injustices going on but was now better able to influence and help make things better.

In 1981 I still lived in Brixton and was in the midst of the riots of that year. I lived in an area called Poets Corner, near the infamous 'Front Line'. By the time of the 1984 riots I had moved out to East Dulwich, but my parents still lived in Poets Corner. Enough was enough – I had seen police brutality for too many years, I needed to do something. I decided to join the police force as a Special Constable. After six months I was a qualified policeman based at Clapham police station, but occasionally working at any of the Lambeth police stations. I needed to understand what made the police tick, why they treated people like this – I wanted to make a difference on the streets of Lambeth.

It was the toughest experience of my life. On the street I received abuse from the white and black communities alike. I was only about 22 years old and still naive and inexperienced in life, so I found it painful. There was worse to come. In the police station or in the vans the police would talk about black people as if I weren't there. They would use the word 'Nigger' when describing people on the street even though I was sitting in the van right beside them. The black people would call me 'white man lover'. They would often say, 'Don't you know they are calling you Nigger behind your back?' The abuse was more difficult to take when it was coming from my own community. These experiences have given me enormous strength of character and resilience in all areas of my life.

I joined the police because I wanted other young black boys to join me in an attempt to make the police force more representative of the community it was meant to serve. I also felt the police might better understand the community if more of us joined. However, due to work commitments I had to give up my part-time role.

After leaving the police I almost immediately became a lay visitor to six police stations: Lambeth, Clapham, Brixton, Streatham, Gipsy Hill and Kennington. The lay visitors scheme was formed out of a recommendation from the Scarman report into the Brixton riots. I had access to any of these police stations at any time day or night, with the objective of checking on the condition of detainees. People in Brixton did not trust the police; they felt that those detained in police stations were being abused. When prisoners were arrested they lost their liberty; unfortunately they were also losing their dignity due to mistreatment at the hands of the police. The scheme was successful and eventually spread to many other boroughs in London and towns and cities throughout the UK. I became vice-chair to the panel of lay visitors and was regularly in meetings with senior police officers to discuss our findings and present ideas for improving aspects of detainees' conditions in police cells. On a monthly basis the lay visitors would make a public statement about detainees in police cells in Lambeth. By doing this we were able to satisfy the public fears which had been instrumental in causing the 1981 and 1984 riots.

Since 1982 not one year has gone by without me actively giving back to the community.

From me to you

As you read the interviews with the role models in this book, Steven and I invite you to see what 'bricks' or experiences in their life stories relate to your own. What can you learn from each individual and, more importantly, what does it tell you about what you want to be and do in your life?

Calling all the ordinary heroes

This book was born of frustration and possibility. For many years I (Steven) have been involved in the field of education, working with young people in schools, colleges and universities and also with BME graduates to assist them in their personal and vocational development. This work is needed because Patrick and the other role models in this book are still the exception rather than the rule.

At all the conferences exploring BME underachievement comes the cry 'we need more visible role models for young people from BME communities'. The absence of positive role models that BME people can relate to is a loss not only to individuals but also to the British BME community.

You can turn on the TV and you might see a black footballer or rapper, but how often do you see black chief executives, or teachers, rocket scientists, etc? Instead the media highlights the conventional stereotypes – if you're black you must be a security guard, DJ, shopkeeper, good at dancing, athletic or maybe even a taxi driver or hospital porter and at worst a criminal or somebody you should avoid by crossing the road if they walk towards you. Why are there no black people in *Friends* and why do the majority of superheroes tend to be white?

Our stereotypes are powerful and often unconscious. They also have very little to do with whether we think we are prejudiced and whether we discriminate. A study at Harvard called the Implicit Association Test* showed people two images simultaneously. They were asked to hit a button saying whether the image was good or bad. The only thing that was measured was the time it took to label something as good or bad. For example, two images were flashed, one of an insect and one of a flower. How quickly the subjects would make a choice was observed by the millisecond. Interestingly 70 per cent of respondents associated white with 'good' and black with 'bad'. Even 49 per cent of black respondents were equally prejudiced towards white being more positive than black. This was unconscious and certainly would not have matched the respondents' self-disclosure of their own prejudices.

Increasingly we are also seeing people being discriminated against because of their faith, which has led to the term 'Islamaphobia'. The problem is that if you happen to look Asian or Middle Eastern, you might be considered a Muslim terrorist or dangerous. Post September 11th, religion has been played upon by racist organisations to an even greater extent than ethnicity in some cases.

One result of these stereotypes or cultural conditioning is that those from BME communities might have limited access to certain professions or roles that fall outside the traditional ones. What happens if the Indian son doesn't want to be a doctor, lawyer or accountant but instead a hat maker or rocket scientist? What happens when the African Caribbean son doesn't want to be an athlete or a church minister but a comedian or an architect? What about the Bangladeshi woman who although a mother of three sees herself as a politician, baroness no less?

Through being on the Windsor Fellowship programme I learned that although I could appreciate my own difference, the reality of life is that many people are afraid of differences and often we don't know the barriers we face because we never get the opportunity to aspire above them.

* Try online at https:/implicit.harvard.edu/implicit/demo/selectatest.html

Perhaps we don't have the language barriers or the economic means or networks that allow us to be part of what those who do take for granted. While at university I had a part-time job at a supermarket. I would wonder about the shelf stacker from Pakistan who had a Master's in Law and a work permit but could not find work. I would be perplexed at how few of the managers were from a minority background and how the higher up you looked, the whiter everyone was.

When I graduated I took a job as a hotel manager looking after recruitment. Again I was struck by the volume of people from visible ethnic backgrounds doing the lower jobs. Chamber maids, waiters, receptionists, many of them skilled but unable to find jobs or have their qualifications recognised in Britain. London gave freedom, but the cost was huge and the wage was minimum. Wherever I looked it was somebody from a minority group who cleaned the street, washed the sheets, kept society going.

At school I would remember how my classmates' parents were doctors, lawyers, one was even a film producer, and how they would do shadowing placements or seem to get the right work experience. I settled for Woolworths where I stacked shelves for a week. Is this what I could aspire to, I wondered? (Nothing is wrong with shelf stacking, it just wasn't what I wanted to think about as my career.) Some of the reasons for BME underachievement are explored after the interviews for those interested in this fascinating area.

However, for now, this book will focus on the positive – not being idealistic but in order to balance the picture by showing that you can be from a BME community and be happy and successful in a wide variety of careers. It is important that the lessons in this book are not only for those who define themselves as BME. This book has something to offer anybody who wants to look at what they value in life and the lessons they have learned.

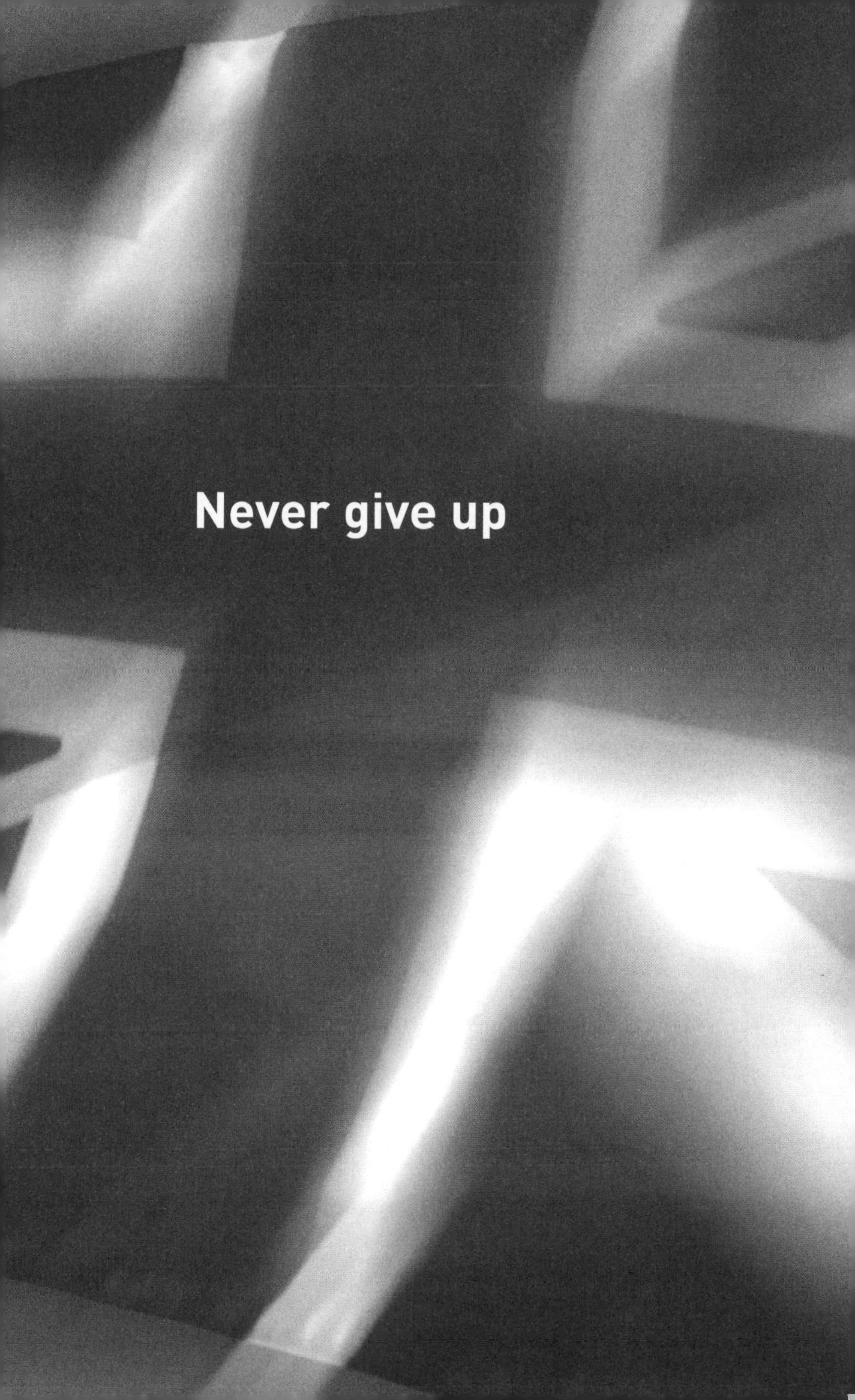

Never give up

An interview with Partha Dey, MD of PDT Express

I am sitting in the lounge of a Luton coffee bar when Partha Dey whisks up to me from my right. Like a sudden gust of wind he appears as if out of nowhere. Dressed casually in blue striped cotton shirt and tanned leather jacket, he insists on buying the drinks. I am taken aback by his energy and also by his goodwill. He is my first interview but already I feel like I am his customer. Although 35 years old, Partha exudes a boyish energy and enthusiasm. It is this spirit of adventure that comes across during the whole interview.

Can you tell me a little about your upbringing or any early childhood memories?

I was born in Luton in 1968 and have lived here all of my life. My parents are from Calcutta and my dad came to England first, went back to India to marry and then my parents settled here. My dad was a horologist and later worked for Kent Meters, and my mother was a sewing machinist at Vauxhall Motors. I really don't have that many significant childhood memories that come to mind. My childhood was happy and our family was content. All my memories are happy.

When did you first notice you had the drive to become an entrepreneur?

When I was 16 years old. I remember I started to become fascinated by business. I would read the business press, magazines and reporting papers such as the *Financial Times.* One day I decided spontaneously to take a train to Central London and I literally walked into the reception of a major investment bank. Without an appointment I insisted to the receptionist that I was not going to go anywhere until they let me speak to a trader. I was just set on making as much money as possible and I wanted to learn how they did it. Eventually a trader came down and let me into a board room. I was in awe of the plush surroundings, the waterfall and marble. If this was what being rich was, I wanted it. The trader told me that if I wanted to pursue a career in his field the best advice would be to follow the educational system and get good qualifications.

How did that meeting influence you?

I started buying shares and investing in the stock market when I was in my first year at university. I had no capital so I borrowed money from banks – as a student I was able to take out a five grand overdraft and I would invest that. It was easy to borrow in the 80s. Soon I was able to buy a car from the profits and then I noticed that my account manager started to buy the same shares as me!

Did you go on to university or go straight into business?

After sixth form I went to Hull University where I did a degree in Electronic Telecommunications Engineering. Not so much because I wanted to become an engineer but because I was good at maths and physics. My parents also thought that engineering was a good field to go into as being a doctor was not a possibility because I can't stand looking at blood. The degree was fine but to be honest I can't really remember too much of it as I was too busy having fun. During my time at university I took three months' holiday and took a plane to Toronto in Canada. I arrived with nothing except a little money to get me accommodation for the night. I ended up doing odd jobs, from envelope stuffing to being a movie extra. Then I decided to hire a rickshaw for $20 a week and sought sponsorship by Labatts Blue. They gave me a tee-shirt and branded trousers and I pulled the rickshaw in down-town Toronto. I was making over $80 each day. Soon I had saved a sizeable amount of money and spent the remainder of the time using it to travel the States. This taught me that I could create money easily but it was hard work too.

Did you go back to university? What did you do after?

Yes. I graduated with a 2:2 and then went back to Luton to train as a chartered accountant with a small firm. I wanted to learn about all aspects of business from VAT to reconciliations to PAYE and felt that a smaller firm would give me a more thorough experience. Yet while working my mind was elsewhere as I started to invest in properties. Within three years I managed to buy three properties, a four-bedroom semi-detached house, a flat and a three-bedroom house, all of which I rented out.

How did you afford to do that?

I had very strict investment criteria and negotiated heavily with the estate agents. I would bring a friend with me to each of the properties. He would be silent with a notepad. In some rooms I would stamp the ground with my foot and he would sigh and write down points, looking very negative. The buyer at this point would think that something was wrong with the house! Afterwards I would go to my own surveyor, the best in town, and tell them how much I wanted the property valued at, which by the way was significantly below the asking price. Surprisingly they all agreed with my offer price. I bought the four-bedroom property for £72,000 down from £100,000 and the three-bedroom house for £32,000 down from £50,000 and finally a two-bedroom flat for £14,500. I was making a profit of nearly £200 a week from rentals.

So was this all a success story?

No. Then what could go wrong did. The properties had 20 reported burglaries within a month. I discovered that one property had an informal reputation as the 'crack house' of Luton and one evening my mother called me and told me that a tenant had been murdered in another property. It could not get worse. Fire, theft, tenants leaving without paying and now murder.

So how did you respond to these events?

I knew that I needed to create another source of income not dependent on rentals. First I went to Calcutta where my parents were on holiday and I brought back to London several samples of portfolio cases and handbags. I travelled the country with them but received no orders. One morning I was in Camden Town and just about to get into my car after another refusal when a Sikh business owner asked me for an exclusive deal and offered me a £5,000 order. I was overjoyed, went back to India and fulfilled my part of the order. When I went to him for payment he said to me, 'not this month, maybe next month'. After a while I realised that he had absolutely no intention of paying me. It took me ten years to recover the outstanding amount, personally serving a summons on him at 5.30 in the morning with a bodyguard and endless days spent preparing for a high court case which I eventually won.

What did you learn from the experience?

This experience taught me the biggest lesson in business: always follow business principles, especially when giving credit. If something does not sound right, it probably isn't. Now I make sure that in my current business we have robust and foolproof credit systems so I don't make the same mistake.

Did you have a debt buying so many goods and having no income?

Yes. I was £18,000 in debt with no money coming in except income from the rentals allowing me enough to live. I decided to put up a poster in the van that I used to deliver the leather goods, saying 'Local Deliveries – Cheapest Rates', and I put an advert in the local newspaper. I drove my van from 6.30 in the morning till 11.30 at night, only stopping briefly to eat a meal in the evening. On average I would do 120 deliveries in one day and make 15–20 collections. Within nine months I had earned £40,000 and cleared off all my debts.

Did you invest further in this business?

Yes, as the profits started to come in I invested in a further two vehicles within two months of each other. Again disaster struck as I lost a major contract when one of my drivers who failed to deliver an item took it home and decided to burn it. The item turned out to be Methadone and I had Customs and Excise banging down the door in the early morning. This certainly required an explanation to my parents who were probably thinking the worst about their son's business then! Luckily I managed to gain other clients and the business has just grown from strength to strength. We are now based at Luton Truck Stop on a 5.5-acre site and we have twelve vans, ten of which we own. I currently have 14 employees and we are one of the leading business-to-business same-day delivery companies in Luton. Our service is second to none in the UK.

With so many setbacks throughout each of your business endeavours, what kept you going on?

I know that I am going to be successful. I don't feel this, I know this. I never look at a situation negatively. For example, one of my vans went missing. Instead of tearing my hair out, I simply focused on what I could do to replace it and recover the cost. I value everything I have, every pound that I earn. I never buy things that I don't need but I enjoy whatever I do spend my money on to the fullest.

How important is your family to your success?

Very. My father died a few years ago but my parents, and particularly my mother, have made my success possible. She always encouraged and supported me, no matter how bizarre or impossible the things I wanted to do. She is there for me and if I need something then she will do it. When I started van deliveries my mum would manage a leather stall in front of the Arndale Shopping Centre in Luton for me. My father was also a big influence on me. He was a very principled and extremely honest man who earned everything he had through hard work. Although he said few words, his quiet energy and human touch commanded respect.

What are some of the passions you have in life?

I am extremely passionate about many things and from the moment I wake up to the moment I go to sleep I aim to live life to the full. I love climbing. In May 1999 I climbed Ben Nevis (1,344 metres up and Britain's highest peak) alone with no equipment or specialist clothing. In the last two years I have climbed Kilimanjaro, Mont Blanc and also reached Everest base camp (circa 5,800 metres). I have also climbed Island Peak (circa 6,200 metres) in the Himalayas. This year I managed to accomplish my pilot's licence, despite the fire alarm going off during my test when I was on the runway. I really enjoy travelling. Some years ago I was out of the country 40 weekends out of 52, often booking a flight on the Internet and figuring out accommodation and practical matters when I was out there. Sometimes I would ride my bike over to continental Europe. I also see myself as a closet singer. My next objective is to be the next Robbie Williams.

[*Having grade 5 in piano and violin and also playing to a high standard the accordion and tabla – touring in a national Asian band – I have no reason to doubt him.*]

Having achieved a measure of personal success, do you feel any form of responsibility to the wider community?

Yes, certainly. I like to help as many people as I am able to. In two days' time I am shaving off all my hair to raise money for the Pasque Hospice, which is a local children's hospice. I am also a member of the Dallow Business Partnership, which aims to help business make contributions towards the local community.

Who are your role models?

I have two who come to mind and they are both climbers and unfortunately have passed away. The first is Goran Cropp, who wrote *The Ultimate High*. I am inspired by him because against all odds he cycled from Sweden to Base Camp Everest and back, a round trip of more than 14,000 miles. The second climber is Anotoli Brokreev, who wrote the book *Above the Clouds*. I admire him because of his humble beginnings in Kazakhstan. Without any essential gear or equipment he was able to climb 8,000 metre mountains and his endurance was phenomenal. My friend Vasant Mepani has also been a role model to me as he has a very creative mind and can find computing solutions with ease. Of course I also have to say Richard Branson. I read his autobiography (*Losing My Virginity*) and I felt some similarity with him in that we both persist and have had to overcome obstacles. For example, on the maiden flight of Branson's first aircraft one of the engines blew. Although on a much smaller scale, the same happened to one of my vans.

What are the three most important factors in your success?

I never ever give in. When I hit the lows I keep going. For example, when I climbed Ben Nevis I was caught in a storm at the top, lost my way and came down the east cliff face. I slipped and hung over a 2,000ft drop. I realised at that moment that unless I am in a life or death situation I can handle all problems and they are simply not so significant. A second factor to my success is that when I set an objective, I hit it. I don't care how long it takes but I stick to it till I get there. An example is when I was doing daily deliveries and I would have a goal to finish the route at four. No matter how bad the day seemed to be or how pushed for time I was, I would always finish on time. The third factor is creativity. I have always tried to be different. I look for what is wrong and then what can be done to provide a solution. Mistakes and problems fascinate me as they give me the opportunity to spot a service. Above all the points mentioned I am also a very high-energy person and see physical exercise and looking after myself as critical to my success. Reflection and capturing my thoughts is also vital. When I started my business, for ten years I would carry a Dictaphone and capture every single thought or idea that came through my mind. I made sure I would listen through each tape before I moved to the next one. This gave me many ideas that perhaps I would have missed.

Do you have any advice for budding entrepreneurs who will read this book?

If you have a dream, make it a reality. Take daily small steps to get there. Break down your long-term goals into medium- and then short-term goals and then each day make a list of what you need to get done. Then simply do it.

What are your goals?

I want to create PDT as a 'National Same-Day Delivery' service. To be able to provide excellent customer service wherever the client is in the UK. Also, before I die I want to have as many life experiences as possible, whether flying, climbing or simply shaving my hair for charity.

Born in Luton, Partha is the Managing Director of PDT Express, a specialist same day UK courier company. Partha is currently involved with two further directorships, one for recruiting for the skills gap in the UK and the other to form a consolidation in the UK same-day delivery market.

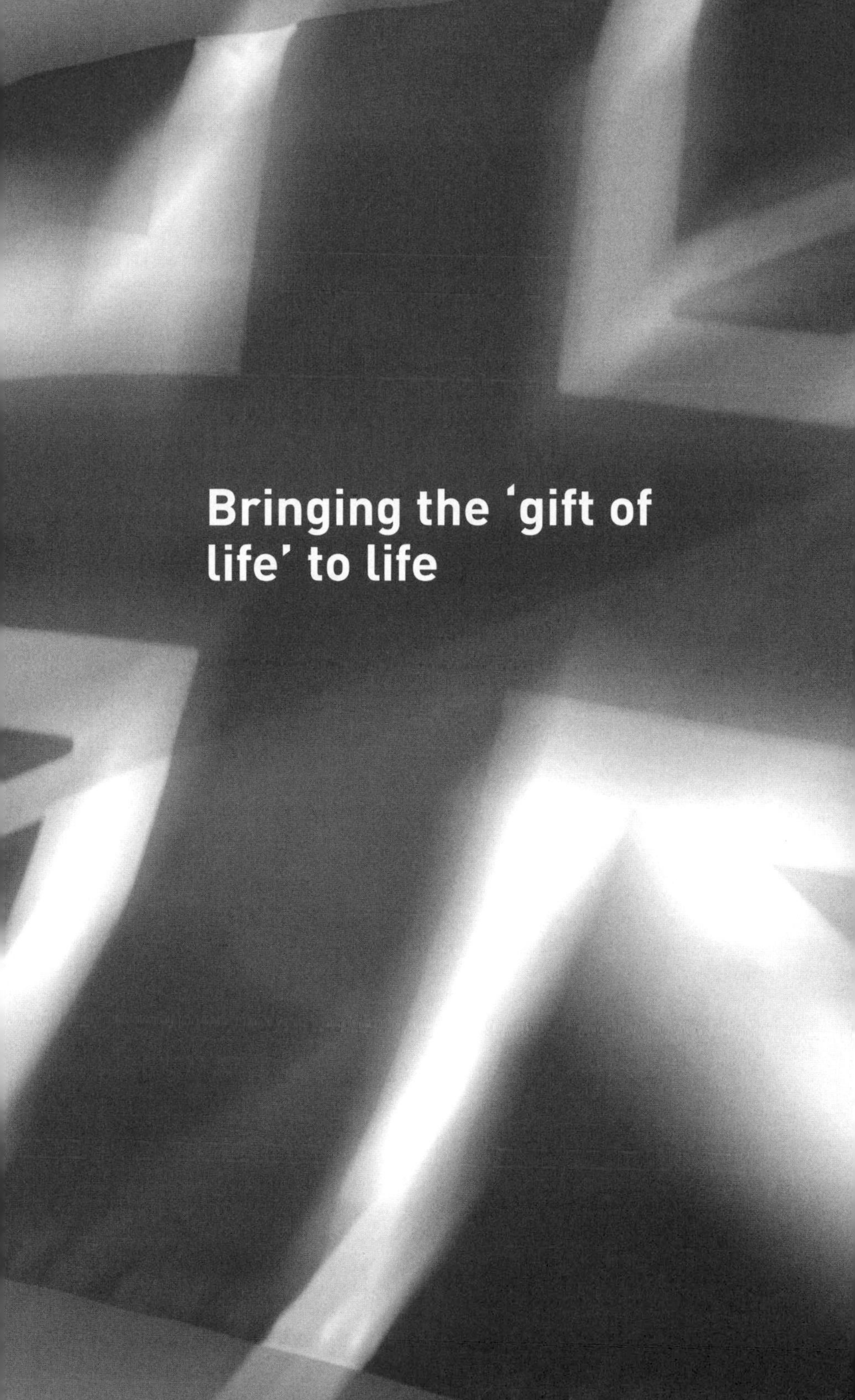

Bringing the 'gift of life' to life

An interview with Beverley De Gale and Orin Lewis

I first met Beverley and Orin at Kensington Town Hall where their son Daniel was speaking to an audience of hundreds of people in the presence of a Cabinet Minister about his triumph over leukaemia. Although Daniel was centre stage, it is his parents who have worked together not only to support him through his illness but also to campaign vigorously and set up a charity, the African Caribbean Leukaemia Trust (ACLT), to support sufferers in the African Caribbean, Mixed Parentage community. Their story shows that with enough passion anything can be achieved and that 'by any means necessary' is a positive statement of never giving up on hope.

Can you both tell me what were the circumstances that inspired you to start the ACLT and why you decided a charity was the best way to do that?

The ACLT was started in 1996, three years after our son was diagnosed as suffering from leukaemia. After receiving two years of chemotherapy treatment he relapsed and urgently needed a bone marrow transplant to survive. In 1996 there were just 580 black people registered as potential donors with the Anthony Nolan Trust. Our son's consultant said that we had a 1 in 250,000 chance of ever finding a match and so we registered ourselves with the Charity Commission and started recruiting black and mixed parentage people onto the UK bone marrow registers in order to find matches not just for our son but for all black and mixed parentage sufferers around the world. We set ourselves up as a charity so that the general public and potential financial donors would take our work more seriously.

Given those starting conditions, what would you say is the biggest achievement to date for the charity?

Well, when we started there were only 580 black people on the bone marrow register. Now there are over 16,500. This is a phenomenal increase given the number of years we have been in operation. Since 1996 eight matches have been found on the register of potential donors, directly through the work of the ACLT. We also consider one of the achievements of the charity is in raising awareness of the issue of bone marrow transplants in the black community and changing perceptions. When we first started, 'giving blood' was considered a taboo subject, it was just not talked about. Now we would be surprised if there is anyone in the black community, especially in London, who is not at least aware of the issues around giving blood and the importance of the bone marrow register.

What were some of the obstacles you encountered trying to set up the charity and how did you overcome them?

We had the personal crisis of looking after our son and the upset of receiving further treatments and talking him through the prognosis. Daily/weekly visits to Great Ormond Street Hospital to receive chemotherapy and various other treatments. Our son having to receive intravenous antibiotic treatments at our local hospital. Also trying to ensure that he was able to attend school to get some sort of education. Additionally, running the charity at the same time as having to travel up and down the country hosting bone marrow registration clinics. Undertaking television, radio, newspaper and magazine interviews to raise the profile of our son's predicament and publicising the venues and dates of up and coming registration clinics. We have a younger daughter (Dominique) and Orin has two sons (Lutalo and Jelani) who all need our love and attention. We also both held down full-time jobs while juggling all of the above.

Can you describe a specific failure/major disappointment? What did you learn and how did it make you stronger?

At the height of our campaigning we were told by the Anthony Nolan Trust that they could no longer tissue type the blood samples because of the amount we were sending through to be tested as possible matches. So we had to get in touch with a laboratory in North Carolina in the United States which agreed to tissue type all our blood samples at a cost of £27.50 for each sample tested. By the time a match was found for our son we had a bill of approximately £87,000 that we were responsible for paying. At times we had to ask ourselves, why should we have to pay this bill? All we wanted to do was to find our son a life-saving donor, surely the NHS, our government, the Anthony Nolan Trust or some other body should be paying this bill? We are not the first family to be looking for a life-saving match for our loved one, are other families told to do the same thing? Anyway, we couldn't ponder and decided to continue until a match was found. On top of everything we decided to take up a massive fundraising campaign, which assisted us in paying off the very large bill.

The ACLT has a motto – 'By any means necessary' – and it helped us not to allow barriers that were put in our way to block our progress. We were fighting for our son's life, so there was nothing that could have stopped us.

What do you consider to have been your greatest moments of happiness/success since starting the ACLT?

Bev's response: Being told by our son's bone marrow consultant that a match had been found, after three years of searching, was certainly one of my greatest, happiest and most successful moments. It is certainly on a par with the bone marrow donation actually arriving at Great Ormond Street Hospital and being delivered into our son's isolation cubicle ready to do its stuff.

Orin's response: In addition to Beverley's comments I would add the moments when I first spoke to Daniel's donor, Doreene Carney, via the telephone on Christmas Eve 2003 and when in April 2004 Daniel opened our hotel room door in Detroit and we actually met Doreene for the first time.

In June 2000 you held the first 'Gift of Life' ceremony. Can you tell me a little more about that?

We held the first Gift of Life fundraising ball a year after Daniel's transplant to celebrate not only his health but also the work of the charity. We also saw it as a way to raise funds and profile the work of the charity and to date it is the biggest event of our year. At the first Gift of Life we had over 320 guests, and celebrities such as Gabrielle, John Fashanu and Ian Wright have hosted tables over the years. The last three years we have held the event at the Intercontinental Hotel in Hyde Park with over 600 guests. The event gives people the opportunity to meet Daniel and to see how our work is progressing. It is an important forum that brings together the sufferers and their families and friends. It's an event that we hope will allow them to switch off from the everyday worries and we try to make it a time to enjoy.

How have you found it working together day in day out as a team?

It has been great working as a team in bringing together a common goal that we have lived and breathed for nine years now. Because our son has achieved his goal it took a lot of pressure off us in a personal sense and allows us to now focus entirely on what the ultimate goals are for the charity.

Where do you get your inspiration and energy from?

Firstly our children and then from the sufferers and their families and carers whom we now assist.

Who are your role models?

Our son is a role model, for his courage and unwillingness to ever accept defeat. He wholeheartedly refused to allow himself to become depressed about his situation and was always seen to have a smiling face and a healthy mind. Thankfully he continues in the same vein. His mind remains focused on what he wants to achieve in life.

Other role models are Muhammed Ali, Nelson Mandela, Oprah Winfrey, Dr Martin Luther King, Malcolm X, Rosa Parks. Many of these individuals have shown great courage and some have been prepared to be imprisoned for their principles and if necessary die to make a difference on behalf of so many others.

You chose the motto 'By any means necessary' for the charity. Why?

The motto comes from Malcolm X and is often quoted with very negative connotations, suggesting unethical means can be used to justify positive ends. We wanted to turn the popular understanding around to make it something positive. When we started our charity we hit lots of metaphorical brick walls. We were told: 'What you're doing won't succeed, Daniel's case isn't unique enough, popular enough to get support.' Orin and I would look at each other and say our motto. We would keep pushing on no matter what. The motto says that we will always show determination and persistence no matter what the obstacles.

How have you helped Daniel live as normal a life as possible?

Our son has always kept his feet firmly stuck to the ground and kept his mind focused on achieving his aspirations and dreams. Throughout the very difficult times all he wanted was to be as normal as all of his mates and so he could almost switch his mind off to the negative side of what was happening and only switch it on when it was necessary. Anyone who meets our son for the first time would never guess what this young man has had to endure because he does not ponder on the past; his head is firmly screwed on to look at the present and future. We are happy that he has this approach to life because we believe it to be a far healthier outlook.

What qualities do you think young people need to make a difference in the world?

Patience, perseverance, assertiveness, desire and respect – not necessarily in this order.

What do you hope to do next with the ACLT?

We would like to get the numbers of black and mixed parentage potential donors on the UK register up to approximately 30,000–40,000 so that if matches are not available from the US register matches will be available for sufferers from the UK register and vice versa.

It would be a dream come true to have an ACLT 'potential donors' database with our own laboratories, tissue typing blood samples and being linked to all the registries around the world. This set-up would allow us to check the world databases for possible matches and allow the world registers to check ours for potential matches. This would be the ultimate scenario for us. However, it would require massive cash donations to make this wish a reality. Still, who knows, anything's possible. As we always say, 'By any means necessary'.

Beverley and Orin, two busy IT professionals, started the ACLT, one of Britain's most significant black charities, nearly 10 years ago. The ACLT are currently working with the National Blood Service (NBS) on a campaign to persuade members of minority communities to give blood. Visit their website at www.aclt.org

Dressed for success

An interview with Asif Kisson

Euston station at rush hour. Hundreds of people walk past but I notice Asif from a long way off. Sporting a distinct black patterned shirt and each individual hair appearing styled to detail, he arranges for a designer who has accompanied him to delay their trip to a London Fashion Week venue so we can fit this interview into what is obviously a hectic schedule. The winner of several notable awards and supplier to Harrods, this is the man who called himself 'a designer with elegance'.

Winning so many awards at such an early stage in your career, would you call yourself successful?

I define success as being not about me but rather the accessories that I create. Designing accessories that make the customer feel very special for their particular occasion is what I define as a success. Each accessory is made to creatively serve my customers' needs. I do not see myself as a role model necessarily, but rather as an example to others that they can create a career doing something that they love, as I have done.

What are your most significant childhood memories?

I have always been interested in nature and sports. At my infant and junior schools I did not really do well at either maths or science but instead found myself fascinated by creative activities, art and design. We used to have nature programmes where we had the opportunity to look at flowers and wildlife. I was taken particularly by the colours that I noticed. In my third year of secondary school I had to make a difficult decision. Did I follow all my male friends and choose to do art and ceramics or pursue my interest in art and fabrics? I knew if I chose fabrics I would be the only guy in a class of 20 and that obviously was not a problem, but it was the teasing from male friends I was more concerned about. The decision was obviously right as I chose to explore fabrics rather than ceramics.

In your biography you mention that you were influenced by chickens. Can you say more?

When I was seven years old our family was offered two chickens as pets. I was really enthusiastic and built a pen for them and a chicken run. What interested me most though were their natural colours. At the time we had a Light Sussex, which was black and white, and I decided to cross breed the hen with a rooster which had brown and silky green feathers. I cannot remember what colour the offspring were but only that at this young age I was interested in natural feathers and the creative possibilities of working with colour.

What inspired your interest in fabrics?

I would have to say nature and the desire to be creative. While at school I never wanted to dress in the same way as the other pupils. The school uniform was black, white and grey and everybody wore the same materials. I would be the only pupil who came in wearing light grey 'Farah's' rather than the usual black flannel trousers. At the earlier age of eight I also remember really liking the Watford football strip. I was intrigued by the colours, even though I definitely did not support Watford.

Who were the most significant early influences on your creative development?

Mrs McKenzie, my textile teacher. She was the person who saw the interest that I had in fabrics and she wanted me to fulfil my potential. She taught me how to use the sewing machine properly and would give me lots of support. Above all she saw my interest in fashion and encouraged me to develop in that direction.

Did you pursue art and design at A-level?

I didn't do so well in my GCSE maths or English so I re-sat those exams. I did not feel that I was ready for further study at that time so I went straight to work in Superdrug in Corby, Northamptonshire. I ended up staying three years. I love retail so the experience was very useful for me. It taught me the importance of customer service, how to deal with people. This experience in serving customers and exceeding their expectations has proved invaluable in my current business.

Why did you leave Superdrug?

It closed down. While working I had been doing sketches and had created a portfolio. I applied to Northampton College and completed a one-year GNVQ in Art and Design before going on to a BTEC diploma in the same subject. I particularly liked the GNVQ as it gave me the room for great exploration of materials. I found that I had a natural interest in techniques to create colour working with materials. In my BTEC course the graphic design element made me more aware of space and the use of negative and positive space to create an effect.

Did you then go on to university?

Usually people assume that I went to Central St Martin's College or the London College of Fashion but instead I chose to study Design Crafts in Carlisle and then transferred a year later to Hereford College of Art and Design. The course in Hereford really interested me as it covered so many aspects such as textiles, ceramics, wood, jewellery and multi-media. It gave me the opportunity to discover what I was interested in as a person.

How did this evolve into the business you run today?

It's directly related. As part of the course we had to set up a project like a business, learning to manufacture according to our own needs. I learned that I design well standing up rather than sitting. I also rekindled my interest in feathers and began experiments in hand-dying natural feathers and then sculpting them into accessories. At the end of the course we had an end-of-year show. Bridget Fraser, the gallery organiser of the

Henley Festival of Music and Arts, asked me what I was going to do with the pieces I had created. She was so impressed she offered me a part in the Henley Festival. At the time I did not realise how big the event was – 25,000 people go to the evening event over four days.

What was your response to such a big event?

This was really my first test in my career, especially to see how the wider public would take to my designs. The response was fantastic – an opera singer wore one of the Cocktail Accessories on the main stage and I sold two to American customers. At the end of a champagne-filled evening it was normal that the guests would pull the Cocktail Accessories from their heads. I received the feedback that nothing broke due to my designs being well made – durable as well as elegant. This feedback encouraged me to explore design as a viable business. I spent nine months researching the market and in April 2001 launched 'Asif Kisson Couture Accessories'.

What do you consider makes your company unique?

We never do any mass production. Each of my designs is a commission piece. The accessories are 1920s styled, both elegant and sophisticated. The detail in each headpiece means that the designs in years to come would be as unique and look as spectacular as they do now. My main creations work on the head and I have personally named them as Cocktail Accessories as I really believe this describes how flamboyant and precious they are. The suede and jewelled feathered Cocktail Chokers are unique and were designed for a lady who would prefer not to wear a hat or a Cocktail Accessory but would simply want a touch of elegance. The piece I am most proud of is a design for a client who got married in Devon Castle, Frances Goddard. Her wedding invitations were covered in beads and a feather delicately wrapped into a bow, and ribbon fastened the invitation just like a scroll, which aroused the curiosity of her guests. I then introduced discretely the same bow into the bride's headpiece and also for the bridesmaids, making it a theme. In spring 2003, Harrods commissioned me as a supplier and I also received orders for the autumn and winter season.

How important is your cultural identity to you?

Both my parents were born in Kingston, Jamaica and I have a few generations going back in Jamaica but my heritage is of North and South India. However, I am of mixed nationalities, as I also have Chinese and European far back in my family history. (There is Chinese on my dad's side of the family and my great-great-great-gran had blue eyes, so there is also European along the way.) My parents came to England in the mid-1960s, first living in London and then moving to Corby where the steel industry was located. Both my brother and sister have English names and I am the only child with an Arabic name. My father was a true cricket fan and I was named after a cricketer. When I liaise with people I do not focus on race, colour or religion; I have experienced discrimination solely based on my name. A few times I phoned shops and as soon as I said my name, their tone of voice changed and I would get an automatic 'No' even before explaining what I do. Overall, apart from my name I do not see my ethnic community as being as important as my local home community, as I do not see race, colour or religion but people and I have a real warming to people in my hometown.

How do you contribute to your local home community?

I was born in Corby, which is a factory-orientated industrial town. Being successful in a creative field, having my own business doing something that I enjoy, I feel can be a source of inspiration to others to follow their own dreams. I have gone back to my local primary school and delivered talks on what I do to classes from 7 to 11 year olds. When I was asked to do a presentation for one hour to a school of 100 kids and their parents, I thought it would be a nightmare. I found instead that the children were really interested due to the colours and designs and I ended up speaking with them for over an hour and a half.

How long does it take to make one of your headpieces?

Each accessory normally takes about three weeks to make as each is individually designed to suit the needs of the customer. Once the design is agreed I need to order the appropriate natural feathers and to hand dye them to the exact colour requirements of the evening. The Cocktail Accessories retail at between £295 and £495 so it still works out to be profitable.

What's next for you?

At the moment I am the events organiser for 'Asian Dreams New Generation' for the show we are doing for London Fashion Week. The event is a catwalk show to support British Asian designers. I am creating a collection of six Cocktail Accessories, which have a romantic and sophisticated feel, and to fulfil this I am working with another designer I truly admire,

Nigina London. It is particularly important to me to have the right music and I am honoured that Urban Dove has kindly created music to complete the whole collection. In the future if I was to partner or work with anybody I could, I would work with Maria Grachvogel because I am a fan of her elegant and chic eveningwear.

Do you have any final words of advice to readers who are thinking of pursuing a career in design or fashion?

If you know what you want to be, instead of working out the steps to your goal think about working backwards from your vision to decide on the courses that will give you the experience you need in order to get there. It is not always necessary to do an academic course but it is very important to network and develop contacts so that people come to you without you chasing them. I always believe it is important to be honest and kind, as you will receive the respect you deserve. Finally, and most importantly, be happy in what you choose as a career.

Asif was born in Corby and after graduating in design launched Asif Kisson Couture Accessories in 2001. His fascination with feathers and intense colours led Asif to the creation of exquisite headpieces and accessories. Each accessory is made to order and he's become a firm favourite with the Ascot and Henley Regatta set.

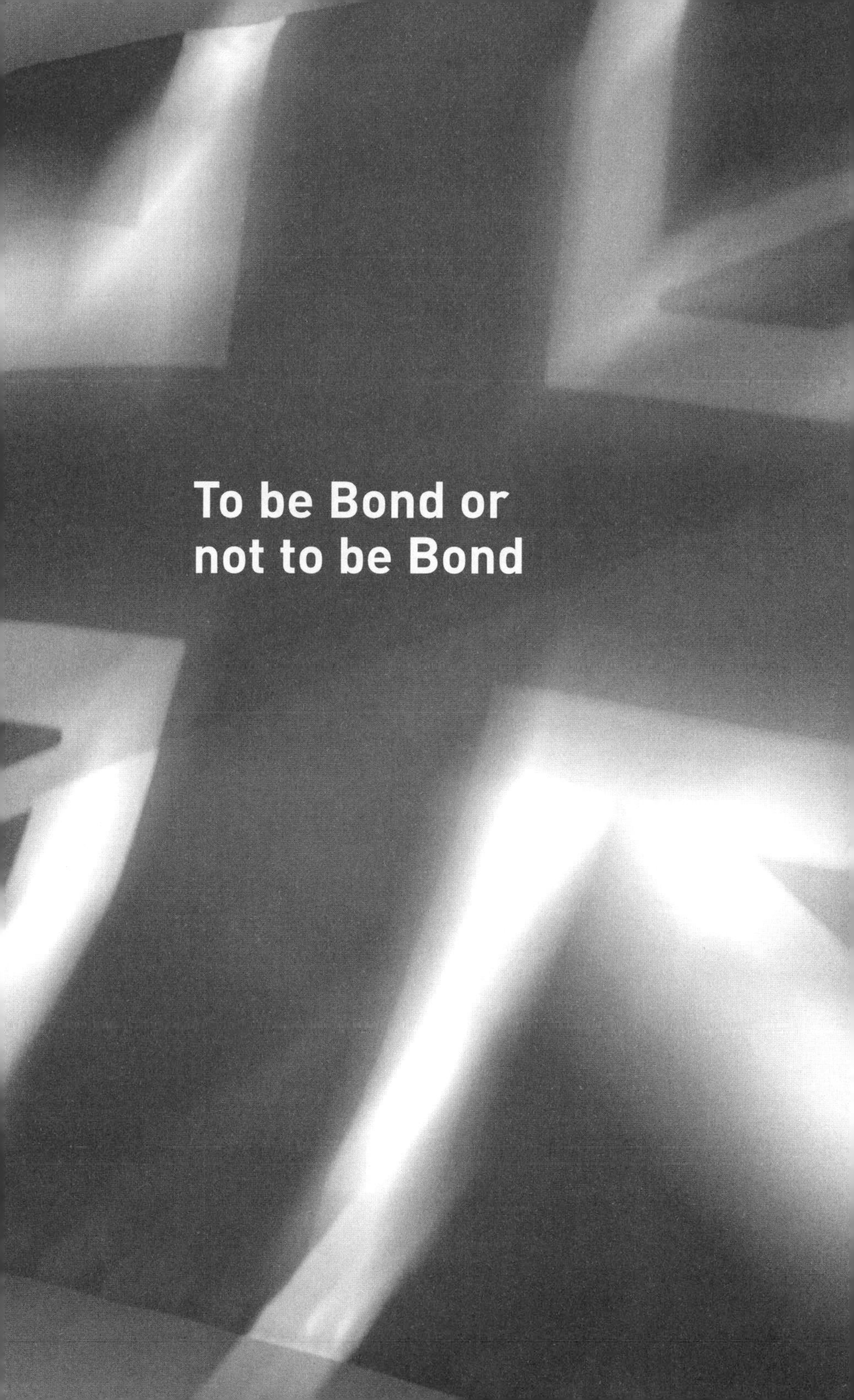

To be Bond or not to be Bond

An interview with Colin Salmon

The first day of spring and I wait for Colin outside Foyles bookshop in Charing Cross Road. He is delayed, caught up in discussing a new film, just one of the many projects being offered to him off the back of media speculation that he might be succeeding Pierce Brosnan as the new James Bond. I had seen him in a recent TV series on the BBC but I had no idea how tall he was in person. Dressed in a fitted suit and shirt, wearing sunglasses and still on his mobile, we make our way to a coffee shop in Soho where knowing time is short I launch straight into the interview. I feel slightly tongue-tied, actually, for the first time, so I stutter out the questions out of the order I had intended.

What are your early memories of school?

I remember my first school very well. I was about four or four and a half and I remember getting awarded lots of gold stars and winning prizes. I did well. It was also confusing as I was the only black person in a 30-mile radius. One incident that sticks out is a sports day in which I was in the running race. I remember racing ahead and reaching the finishing line but rather than go through it I stopped just before. I was scared to break it. Everyone was screaming at me to go through it but instead I went under. That's the story of my life!

Coming from a mixed racial background, did this have any effect on you growing up?

My dad is from Jamaica but my blood father is from Ghana. They say that blood is thicker than water, but I say deeds are thicker than blood. My Jamaican father fed me, bought me my first football boots, brought me up, so to all extents I consider him my true father. My dad is Indian Caribbean, that's very important for me to stress.

I had to come to an understanding of myself due to what I learned at school. I was excluded from school and felt I had to hunt for my identity. Malcolm X and jazz music were both important to me in reaching this understanding. After the third reading of Malcolm X I realised that this wasn't my story and that I hadn't read it yet as I was living it. It was still a powerful experience. I have come to the point where I celebrate my complexity, the world is my family. I don't touch bigotry or prejudice. It is hard for me to see it as it offends and angers me.

Why were you excluded from school and how did you respond?

At the time I was head boy of Ashcroft High School in Luton. I was doing very well at my studies but during my O-levels I became complacent. I failed and had to re-sit. I was thrown out of school only because on one occasion I forgot to deliver letters on behalf of the headmaster. They were to do with his retirement. My mother, who was white and working-class, never got the opportunity to appeal. I think we have explored oppression in the black community but there is also a lot of discrimination that goes against the white working-class community. Do we have to suffer bows and arrows or do we take up arms?

Do you have a role model who has had an impact on your life?

My role model is a combination of my wife, who is incorrigible, dedicated and disciplined; my dad, who was patient, brave, just solid; and Malcolm X. His story speaks to me because he went through so much pain but took the extreme reaction to find himself in the brotherhood of man, black or white. He actually chose a new name to reflect this change of identity, El-Hajj Malik El-Shabbazz. The fact that people still refer to his old identity shows that perhaps they don't grasp the fundamental change that he went through. He went through the same pain that you might go through seeing people in your class driving cars while you are unemployed simply because you have a different skin colour. It might not be their fault and I'm not saying it is, but this happens.

How do you challenge racism?

I am the chair and a governor of a nursery school. The battle is with our children. My vision is that all adults of every colour will one day link arms and all the children will play safely behind them. I challenge racism by fighting for education for our children, campaigning for nurseries and schools to continue providing services that our children need.

I read in an interview that you give talks at local schools. What are the key messages you give?

Be aware that arrogance and confidence are very close. One is the product of fear and insecurity and ultimately dismissive. The other one is quiet and has the knowledge and inner confidence to say 'I don't know'. It is strong enough to defer. There is no need to be a head boy with confidence, the quality of strength is within.

Manners, grace and respectfulness will get you further than you can imagine. Further than any gun. People will warm to you. The true teachers in society are pensioners. When they can see that you have passion and respect they will teach you. You can see this in jazz with all the masters.

Fix up! Look smart. Don't score points over each other. Someone else's defeat is not your victory. Celebrate your friend's success – as one goes up we all go higher.

I see problems as maths. One of my teachers said that the hardest problem was getting on to Marble Arch roundabout. I once gave a talk at a conference on crime which was about black-on-black violence. I remember I tore up my notes and just told them the first occasion I experienced black-on-black violence was when I was four and my father took his belt to me. I brought it down to reality, to what I had experienced. This is what goes on in every community and we can't turn a blind eye and not face facts. For example, in Darfur, 10,000 people are dying a month. Do we know about this? My message is, put your television magazine down, be selective.

Crime is one thing that angers and hurts me. It also affects everyone and is not the problem of only one community. Boys aged 11–16 are more liable to be stabbed, attacked or mugged than many other groups. Their prison is the street. Arrogance is a powerful front that they have to put on in order to survive in their communities. It's not a choice. Education of these young people does affect everybody's children. On Saturday, even if your children go to public school, they are still out on the high street. Some people in South Africa are so afraid of crime that they have armed response teams ready. It is not the white person's fault either. Imagine if they are attacked. Tomorrow your brother might be going for a job in their company. Violence is not an answer. I don't think people want this for everyday life. There is a price and we are all responsible, everyone has an impact.

What needs to happen for more black people to enter the British film industry?

Include yourself. Get a camera and learn to use it. The film industry is relatively young, less than 100 years old. Theatre is something completely different. You've just got to do it. Sit in a room and write it. Walk alone. Jazz proves that this can be done. Many films are just about economics, but you can still tell the truth. Great art appeals at all levels. If you really want to get a message heard, make sure that children can listen to it. It has to reach them.

The important thing is not to think that somebody is sitting in a room thinking of ways to keep you down. They don't care enough. Successful white children don't waste time thinking of racism. Why should you spend time on this?

If something goes wrong and you are treated unfairly, tell someone. Parents really have to listen to their children. Violence is a language that you mustn't teach your children. To channel your energy, learn a martial art. Remember, boys start wars, men end them.

Breakthroughs can occur at any time. I was busking for three years, playing the trumpet. I was spotted by a white man who was passing the Tricycle theatre. These things do happen.

What do you consider your biggest personal and professional success?

My biggest personal success is being the father to four beautiful children who are balanced, kind, bright and talented. It has to be that.

Professionally, I am proud that I am respected as an actor and as a man. What's most important is to be brave and bold in whatever you do. I feel that I have made good choices. Doing this hasn't got me the biggest house on the block, but so far so good.

What do you consider your biggest failure?

My biggest failure is believing that a leopard can change its spots. I cannot help but go back again and again and encourage people. I live in hope. It's not a false hope but I have been disappointed by other people. I don't think I have the energy to keep on doing this. Eventually I will have to say, back off.

What is your favourite film?

Not One Less by Zhang Yimou. In the film a very young teacher, 13 years old, in a poor rural Chinese village is given responsibility for a class of 40 children on the condition that she looks after each and every one of them. In the film one of the boys goes missing and the teacher goes to find him in the city. For me the film is about purity of heart and is also an example of God.

What would you do if you were not an actor?

I would like to be a head teacher. It's a part I play in the drama *Hex*, which is fun. I know my role would be in education. It has to be the most important field. Apart from my acting I am also a trumpet player and play professionally. I act because I just like words too much.

Colin has appeared in the last three James Bond films as well as Alien vs. Predator, Resident Evil *and numerous TV programmes including* Prime Suspect 2, Silent Witness *and recent Sky One drama,* Hex. *In addition, Colin can frequently be found on the London stage.*

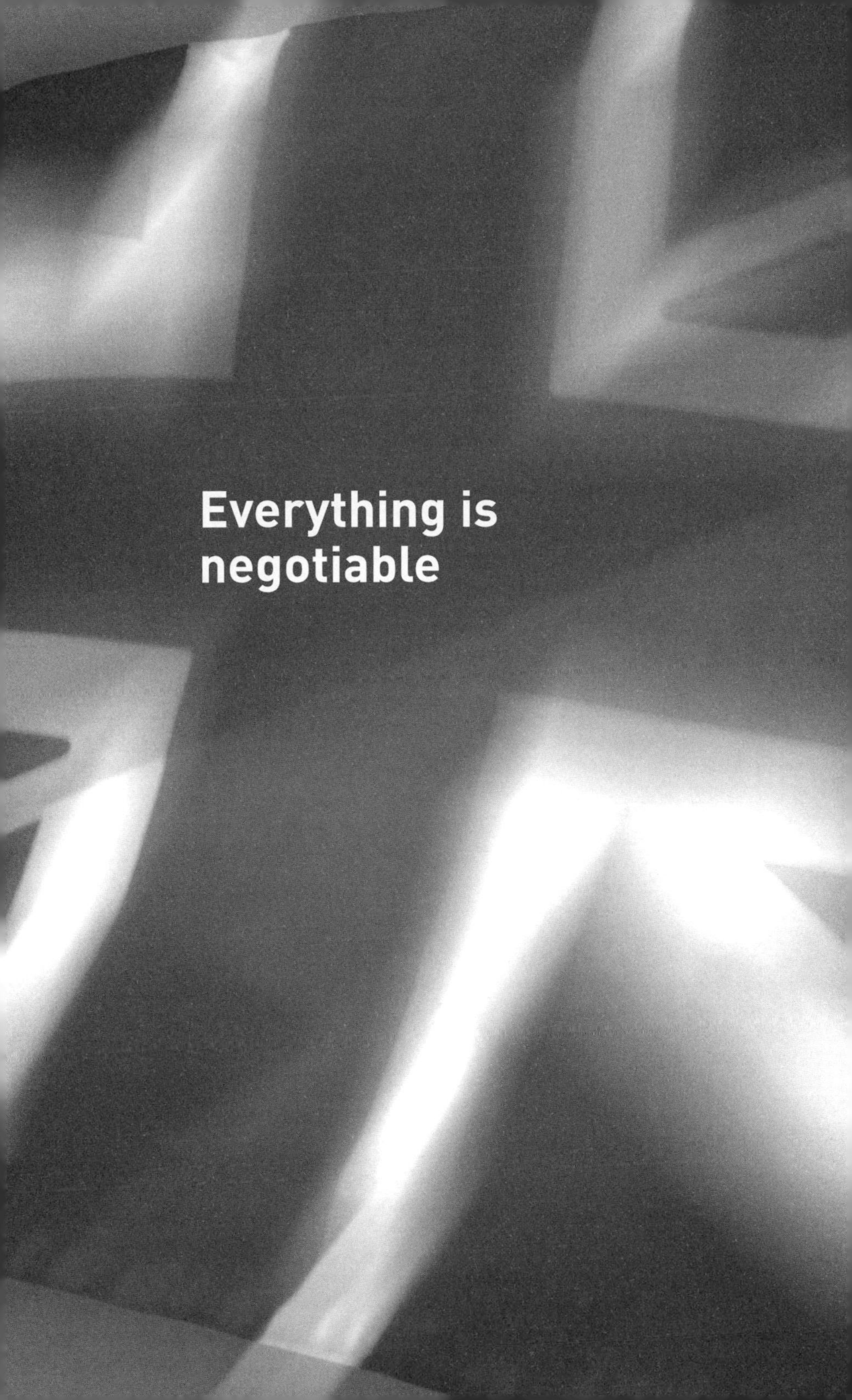

Everything is negotiable

An interview with Bill Morris

I arrive at a St James' address, temporary home to the Morris Inquiry (an independent inquiry into professional standards and employment matters in the Metropolitan Police Service). Taking the lift to the top floor escorted by a security guard I see Sir Bill Morris, head of the inquiry that bears his name, hard at work at his desk. It is barely 8am but he appears to have already broken ground that day. Light fills the spacious office and files bearing the names of well-known media profiles line the wall near the window, a 'who's who' of people Sir Bill will be reporting on. As he speaks, every word is weighed and purposeful, yet they come out effortlessly. During the interview his humbleness, wisdom and social commitment come through clearly but in a way that engenders respect not only for what he has accomplished but for who he is.

What gets you up in the morning?

Knowing that I have a fulfilling life. It has challenges and provides me with opportunities that give me satisfaction.

Having achieved so much in your life, do you feel yourself to be a success?

Success means different things to different people. Some people feel that bringing up children well is a success or achieving a particular ambition. My definition of success is achieving goals that you set for yourself. This could be personal development, climbing a mountain or helping someone. Determining goals and achieving them in business, the community or one's own life is success.

How important was your upbringing on your present success?

Critical. My upbringing was in a small rural community. This shaped my life values: respect, tolerance, collectivism and community. It helped me realise that there is something called 'society'. It also engendered the values of caring and sharing, whether this was knowledge or material goods. I feel that I have had a privileged life and hence have a responsibility to share what I have been given with others.

My family has played a critical role for me. They have been a support and a shoulder to cry on and lean on when necessary. I look to them to do the undoable things and they are the people who see me at my best and worst. They are the abiding spirits and the motivating factor in good and bad times.

Do you have any memories from childhood that stand out?

Just being a happy child in a tranquil and caring environment. I knew no fears, had no worries other than just getting home and to school. These were really golden days and I recognise them when I look back. Those days were materially minimalist – we had no great toys like children might nowadays. Instead our toys were self-made, we had conversation and played with trees. I would not trade any of those childhood days with what children have now, designer trainers, Game Boys. The whole process of evolution is naturally evolutional and each generation has to take the best of the previous to the environment of their time. In 30 years' time people will look back at the fun they had with text messages. It is not about comparing but evaluating.

Who has been your most significant role model?

Miss Sewell. She was quite petite but a little bit tyrannical. She was a tough disciplinarian, but fair, inspirational and leading by example. At primary school she taught me all the subjects but most of all she taught me cricket. Sir Frank Warren could not play better! She had a 'can do' spirit. If I wanted to do something she said, 'Yes you can, yes you will'. This instilled a spirit of self-belief and a stairway of confidence. When she told you that you could get to the top of the stairs it gave you the confidence to do so. I will never ever forget her.

What are you most proud of?

My life has been littered with highlights. The things I am most proud of is being re-elected a second time as General Secretary of my union. The re-election was clearly not due to fortune but showed that what I had achieved was damn good and judged on my record. My re-election validated my first period in office.

What do you consider your greatest failure and how did you deal with it?

I have some personal failures. My biggest was my failure to communicate effectively with my wife when she was diagnosed with breast cancer. Even during the period when it became fatal I felt that my job was to cheer her up rather than depress her. I would not face up to the reality and I have regretted this ever since.

In my career I regret that I didn't take bold and courageous steps to merge my union with another. I played a defensive game rather than being adventurous and take a risk. I was not prepared to take a financial risk and in hindsight I should have done.

You learn from experience. No two situations are exactly the same so you cannot transfer or read across to some future situation. It is also probably not right to do so either as it is dangerous to make pre-judgements. Some principles are constant but the best way to proceed is to judge each set of circumstances on relevance.

How important are risks?

Risk is one of the constants of our lives. Even if we cross the road, we could suddenly get severe cramp and come to harm. Life is full of risks, we need to assess and then to manage the risks. It is important to evaluate. We are constantly risk managing. If you have the extra cup of tea before you take the train you run the risk of hitting all red lights on your way to the station and missing the train. All life is risk.

Trevor Phillips spoke of a 'snowy peaks' syndrome in the senior civil service. Do you feel that the government is doing enough to promote minority ethnic advancement?

Society is formed by a combination of rights and obligations. Young people have an obligation to equip themselves to take up opportunities for personal development, education and citizenship. While they have rights to be heard, educated and to health, they also have obligations. You can't win the race if you don't enter. There is no need to enter a marathon if you have not done the right amount of training yourself. If you put on your trainers on the morning of the race, you simply cannot compete. Young people need to prepare and position themselves so they can compete in all circumstances, job wise and education.

The government needs to recognise the cohesiveness of society is itself a significant investment. An unstable society is not at peace with itself, does not give of itself and it is costly to deal with the problem. The government has the responsibility to create the framework and set the agenda on principles of equality, valuing people, respecting them and their contribution. There is no point in sending people to university and then that they cannot get a job. The government has to create the strategic framework to develop the potential of all, black or white, young or old.

Who are your role models?

I'm an individualist. I never seek to emulate anyone and I just want to be me. There are people I admire immensely and lots of people inspire me. When I was on the shop floor in the Midlands I was very impressed by the chair of the Shop Stewards

Committee. He had an inspirational home-spun philosophy, which guided the way that we worked and kept us motivated.

On the political stage I have been inspired by Nelson Mandela and his ability to rise above adversity. Martin Luther King Junior also inspires me. Both are people who put the cause above themselves and their cause was bigger than the individual.

What is your favourite book?

Nelson Mandela's autobiography, *Long Walk to Freedom* is one of my favourite books. I also am a romantic at heart. I like the poetry of Claude McKay, a Jamaican poet, especially his poem 'Spanish Needle'. The words create an image of tranquillity that takes me back to the Caribbean. I could spend a day listening to his words and daydreaming.

What do you do to gather energy and relax?

I am a home addict and I like spending time at home. This is probably because I am starved of it as I travel a lot. My big moments of downloading everything are at home. My home is a modest place but it is my castle. I sit on the carpet and eat my beans on toast. It is my place of sanctuary, where I feel protected and that no one can touch me there. When I need to solve a problem I go for a run. I take a situation with me mentally and think about it as I work out. I regularly go to the gym to work out.

Sir Bill was born in Jamaica, arriving in Birmingham, England in 1954 and working his way through the ranks of the Transport and General Workers' Union to be elected as Britain's first black General Secretary in 1991 and 1995. He retired from that post in October 2003.

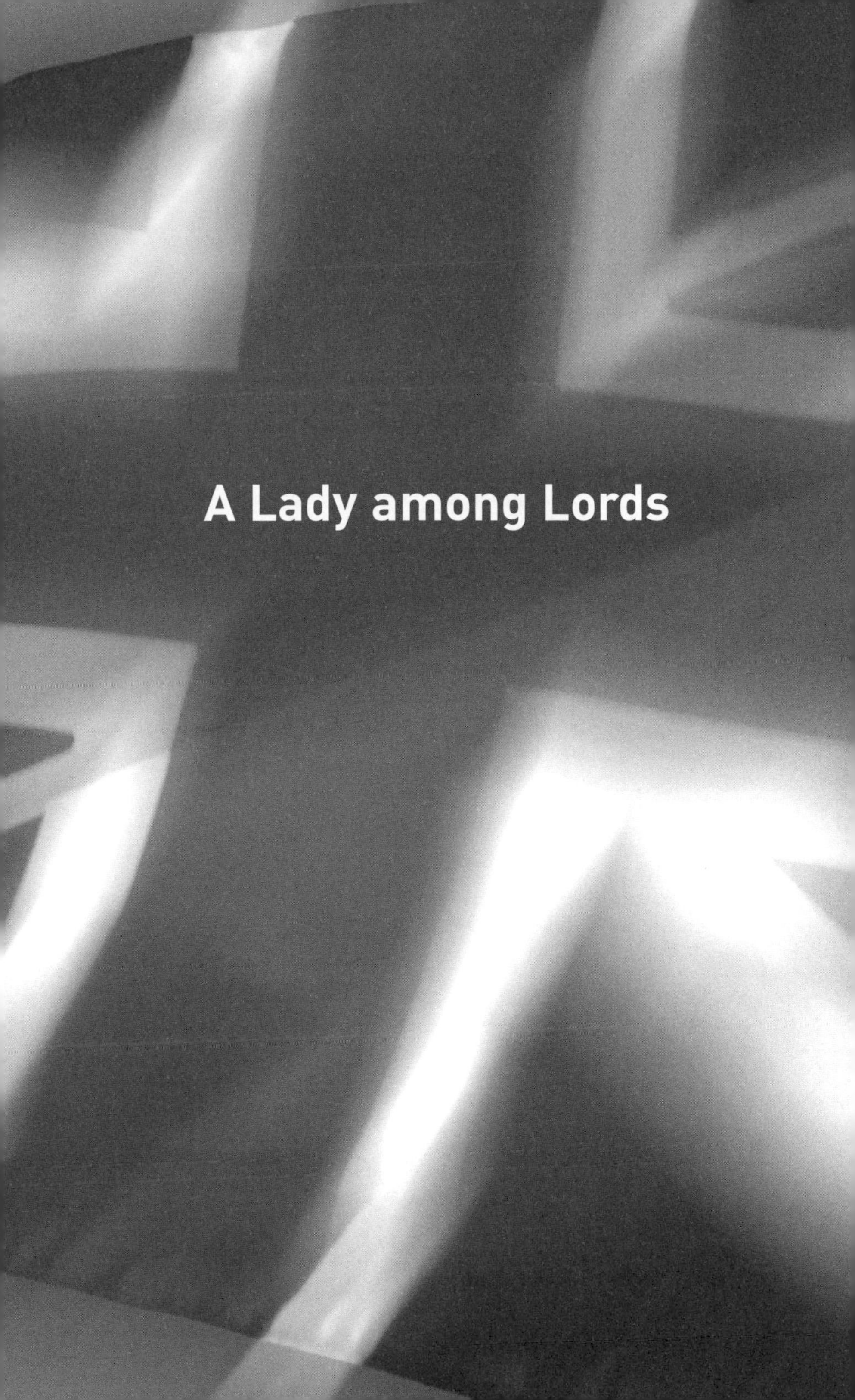

A Lady among Lords

An interview with Baroness Uddin

When it comes to sitting in a waiting room, No. 7 Millbank Place has to be one of the most interesting. I chatted with the police officer on duty as in and out of the revolving doors came Lord this and Lady that. Suddenly a bell rang loudly and several people marched out of the building in a rather unLordly and Lady-like fashion. I found out from the security guard that they were going across the road to the Houses of Parliament to vote. The bell went several times while I was there. My first meeting with Baroness Uddin was as she dashed out of the building, assuring me she would be back.

Can you tell me a little about your upbringing and any memories you have from childhood?

As I was growing up I was fortunate to have had a large extended family around, both on my mother's and father's side. I also had a very warm relationship with both my grandfathers, and my paternal grandfather was my bedrock. We had strong and fantastic women in my family. Other strong memories are the daily walks beside beautiful Padha River with my grandfather, playing cricket with countless cousins and also the importance of our Mashjid. I remember being someone extremely confident and I cannot recall any barriers to being ambitious with my career. Everyone expected me to be a doctor. I was frequently in trouble with my mum for not doing this and that.

What was your experience of school?

My mother was a teacher in Bangladesh and when we arrived in Britain it was made clear to me and my brothers and sister that we had to learn English quickly. We did, which I think made a significant difference to us in our learning.

I was a really good student. I can remember getting lots of prizes in my school. Arriving in Newham in East London at the age of 13 was a total contrast to the experience of schooling in Bangladesh. The teaching was alien and I remember often being reminded that we could not aspire to be lawyers or doctors because our English was not good enough. Our living conditions at the time were very cramped in comparison with the magnificent space I had left behind in Bangladesh, so I hankered after attending school every day, just so that I would get out of our living space. At school the person who most made an impression on me was a Jewish New Yorker English teacher. She believed that I could do well and had good arguments for continuing in education whenever I was downhearted by the discouragement of some very unprofessional and bad teachers. I was fortunate to have her pushing me. While in Bangladesh everyone took it for granted that education in England was the best in the world, yet it was so apparent to me that it was not equally available for everyone, especially for Asian girls.

Did you finish school and then go on to further education?

I was the first person in my family *not* to finish my education. Instead I got married and put my education on hold. This was very unusual in my family, and everyone disapproved. All my cousins had degrees; I had kids! It was around this time that I became involved actively in the community and also with the Labour Party. I got sidetracked in Tower Hamlets, putting my education on hold and becoming involved in the affairs and challenges of that community instead. I was determined to return to study, however, and when my third son was three, I decided to go to university and completed my social work qualification. On reflection I should have gone into teaching; my mother's side of the family is full of teachers and I think it's a great way to influence people. Secretly I think I am a closet teacher.

After you completed your social work course you became actively involved in local issues and community groups. What drove you to participate in these types of activities?

My relationship with Tower Hamlets began when I married my husband, Komar Uddin, without whom I would not have survived in my work. He was living in that area with his family. The area was well known for fascist activities, with the regular presence of the BNP members parading their filth and disturbing extreme materials against the minority community living in the surrounding Brick Lane area. It was menacing. The Bangladeshi families lived in fear and the inequality was all pervasive in the way people were treated, the housing they lived in and the condition of the places where they worked. It was in complete contrast to the idea of England I had grown up with. I had just come from Bangladesh with memories of civil war fresh in my mind. I knew I would not tolerate injustices of any kind, especially if I was to live here. So I believe that it was inevitable that I would become involved in the struggle against prejudice, racism and inequality.

I was very fortunate that I was able to utilise my post as a community worker for the YWCA to engage in developing many innovative projects which promoted access to training, education, housing and employment. Without the people I met and worked with in Tower Hamlets I would not have become the person I am today, and their energy was my inspiration.

How did you become a Baroness?

Throughout the early 1980s I was encouraged by many colleagues and friends to become even more involved. As a result of this involvement I was asked to become a councillor to which I finally succumbed in 1988. At this time the borough was being run by the Liberal Party and we in the Labour movement regarded their policies as racist and divisive, deeply dividing the communities against one another. I felt I could do better. During the 1980s we were collectively involved in many protests and marches against institutions which was regarded as neglecting the needs of ethnic minorities. I believe we changed many organisations and their behaviour as result of our efforts. I had young children and remember dragging them to events and meetings although they would be tired and sometimes bored. I do think these experiences would have made some impact on their attitudes towards understanding different people. Despite being very active in different community organisations, I had not ever wanted to become a councillor and if my recollection is right I think it was regarded as a bit of a 'sell-out'. This period in Tower Hamlets was extremely exciting and many men and women from the community worked together to build on the many successes we enjoy today.

During this time I was also struggling with my son who is autistic. It was an ongoing battle with the local education authority. I was always looking for a better standard of education and services for him, but the institutions involved in the arena of special education were not ready for my kind of argument about equal services for people with disabilities. They continued to believe in segregated provisions while I was arguing for 'mainstreaming' 20 years too early. I was asking for things in the 1980s that we now take for granted and see as our right. At that time people used to say to me that I was 'too ambitious' for my child and almost that I was demanding above my station. To them I was an Asian woman, a Muslim mother who had no knowledge of special needs. Parental rights was not a concept familiar in the field during the early 1980s.

One day a colleague put my name forward for the list of prospective councillors. I remember laughing at the suggestion. The room was full of young people and youth workers and he assured me that nothing would come of it and the Labour Party had to have some women's names on the list. I was the most active woman in the party and he said, 'If anyone rings about it just say no'. Although I didn't want to become involved in what I had regarded as 'dirty politics', I can clearly recall the man's arrogance and that impression was greatly responsible for my final decision to accept the first invitation to address one of the wards when I was invited for a selection meeting. When I stood and won the seat in Shadwell, I ousted a well-known male councillor who had been in that position for 28 years! And that was that. Within three years I became deputy leader of the Tower Hamlets Council when we defeated the Liberal Party and took power. Subsequently I contested the Bethnal Green and Bow parliamentary seat and was not selected, but on Labour returning to power after 18 years out of office, Tony Blair invited me to the Lords. The rest is history, as they say.

Can you describe what you do in the House of Lords?

The House of Lords is one half of our parliament and is called the Upper Chamber. Members of the Lords represent State and Queen. Each member of the House is nominated by the Prime Minister and appointed by Her Majesty the Queen. It is the place where every piece of legislation goes through to become law. It's where bills become law. Sometimes legislation begins in the Commons and ends in the Lords, but it can also start in the Lords. The Lords is also the highest court in our country, although as you may know we are soon to enjoy a separate judicial system.

For me it has provided a great platform and space to continue my activism. During my seven years I hope that I have been able to be a bridge between the people of my area and parliament. Of course I have also had to take up the mantle of the Muslim women and community because the number of Muslims in Parliament is so unacceptably low. Although the members of the Lords do not represent a constituency, as the first Muslim to enter the Lords you are always reminded that you are a voice for the millions of British Muslims. This sometimes seems unfair, although I hope I have honoured that responsibility to the best of my ability. I have also been able to travel to many parts of the world, representing Britain in different meetings and conferences. Both sets of responsibilities can be extremely challenging, especially when you are with colleagues who do not appreciate the challenges of your role.

Do you have any regrets or failures?

My biggest regret is the time I spend away from my children. Changing society provides a great promise of reward, a deep sense of honour and privilege, but once in that role it is often impossible to get out. Serving the community is endless and for women activists, especially ones with a large family, the decision to be away from either duty is sometimes tortuous.

What do you think needs to happen for more representation of minority ethnic people in the House of Lords?

We have to learn the lessons of history and to make our presence felt. Each of us should have the right, simply to serve in Parliament as an individual, not representing any communities, but I realise that is not possible given that the representation in Parliament of Muslims is so dismal. I hope that the British Muslims will take the good examples and successes of the Black and Jewish community in order to increase their presence in Parliament and other institutions. I remain very concerned that at such critical time, we have a long way to go to achieve positions of power and influence. I am deeply frustrated at the pace of change. We focus too narrowly, often giving too much energy to 'back home' politics and not enough to make British institutions accountable. Equally, I am sad to say that our government has also not done enough to utilise the talents of our communities.

Who would you say is your role model?

My involvement in community work and subsequently at a national level in Parliament is purely down to the inspirational and supportive role of my husband and my children. They are my true heroes. I am often asked this question and my answer is always that I need not look any further than the women of my family to inspire me, although during the past thirty years I have encountered a fantastic array of women whose tenacity to survive adversities has been awesome. It gives me hope and reaffirms my belief that each of us, no matter how small our effort, can make a huge impact on the society in which we live.

What are you most proud of?

I am proud of my family and that they have continued to be my inspiration and strength. Also that I have survived, against all the adversities and opposition I have encountered.

Baroness Uddin began her political career in Tower Hamlets, becoming the first Bangladeshi woman councillor, and when elevated to the peerage by the Prime Minister in 1998 she was the youngest woman on the government benches. More recently Baroness Uddin has specially focused on 'Women's Voice' encouraging women's participation and contribution in all aspects of life.

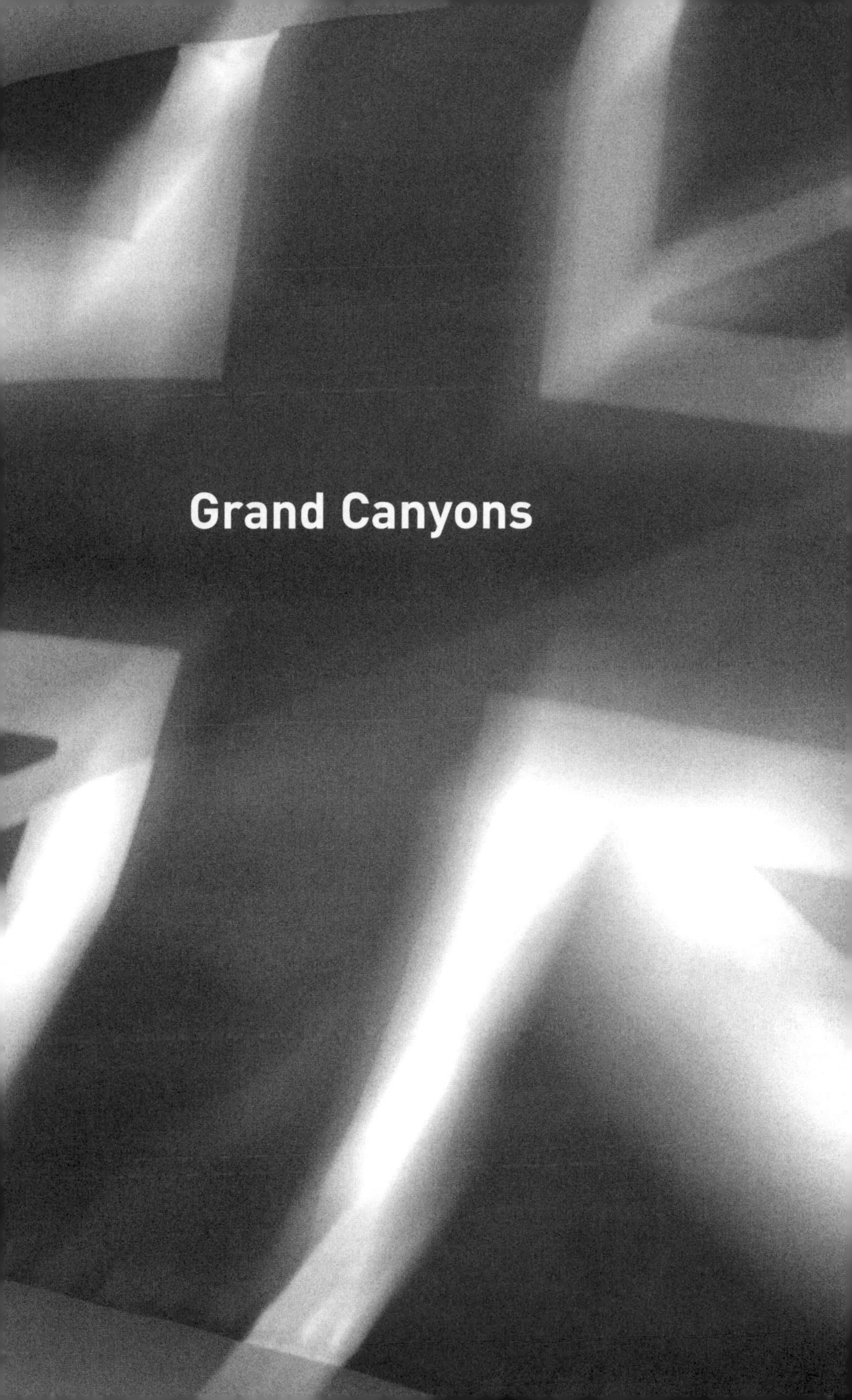

Grand Canyons

An interview with Karan Bilimoria

Karan is a man who makes decisions fast. As the chief executive of one of the world's fastest growing drinks companies, he needs to. His passion for both his product and his staff comes through as he excitedly shares his 'Grand Canyon' plans for his company's growth. In fact the Grand Canyon would be an excellent way to think of Karan. He is a man with huge vision, commitment to the community and to education and entrepreneurship. Much more than a businessman, Karan is also an educator and a family man who makes a difference for all those around him.

How do you define success?

To me, aspiring and achieving against all odds, with integrity, defines success.

What are the top three 'must-have' qualities an entrepreneur needs?

When I first came to Britain I was told that as an Asian, if you wanted to succeed there was only so far you could go before you hit a glass ceiling. What I have come to learn, from creating Cobra Beer from scratch and in the most competitive beer market in the world, is that if you have the passion, drive and aspiration to succeed, the sky is the limit. If you are passionate about your product and have a clear goal from day one, as in my case to 'produce the finest ever Indian beer and to become a global beer brand', and if you are creative and innovative and produce a product that is different and better, delivering a genuine benefit to today's global consumers who are increasingly more demanding and quality-conscious, you can be a success against all odds and change the marketplace.

My business principles have also contributed to Cobra's success. From the outset they have been and remain very straightforward: the product comes first; strive to be different and better and therefore change your marketplace; never ask for exclusivity; treat suppliers and customers alike; maintain an informal yet professional office atmosphere; continuous training programme for all our team; community support; being outward looking.

My ten steps to growth have also been key to my success.

My steps to growth:

1. Research and understand your market thoroughly. Find a niche and fill the gap. Have a clear goal right from the beginning.
2. Improve a product or service – be different and better and change the marketplace forever. Build a brand if possible and add value and build value.
3. Lead, do not follow.
4. Be innovative and creative. You have to come up with the ideas; however, always get consumer feedback, listen to your consumers and be close to your consumers.
5. Constantly look into the future and this means that in business one has to be flexible and adaptable to change.
6. Be passionate and proud of your product or service. Do not compromise on quality or try to cut corners as today's consumers have greater awareness therefore demand better and better quality.
7. You will need:
   a. Focus
   b. Commitment
   c. Drive
   d. Hard work
   e. Sacrifice.

   And never give up.
8. Invest in your people and build a great team. Work with the best advisors – they may be expensive but you get what you pay for.
9. Balance responsibility with growth and be outward looking.
10. Aspire and achieve, although it will probably always be against all odds.

How important was your upbringing to your present success?

My family was, and continues to be, incredibly encouraging and supportive of me. My mother's grandfather, Dinshaw Dadabhoy Italia, has always been my inspiration and his motto was to 'aspire and achieve'. Back in India, he built a large business from scratch starting with a *desi* (country) liquor business in Warangal and then expanding into other areas such as an enamel and porcelain factory, cinemas and property. He was a member of the Rajya Sabha, a Member of Parliament in India, equivalent of the House of Lords. His dynamic and entrepreneurial spirit, marked by his generosity, was such that nobody had a word to say against him. The Parsi community traditionally has a reputation for being honest, decent, straightforward and fair minded, and he embodied each of these values, values which were instilled in me and which I continue to carry each day. 'To aspire and achieve' fell into place for me when I was attending Cranfield University's Business Growth Programme when I added, 'To aspire and achieve against all odds, with integrity', which is Cobra's vision.

What is your most significant childhood memory?

Being with my father when he was Commanding Officer of the 2nd/5th Gurkha Rifles, Frontier Force, as an eight-year-old. The battalion had won three Victoria Crosses in the Second World War. My father's Regimental Sergeant Major was one of them, a living hero, and I fought my first boxing match against his son, who was four years older than me, in front of the whole battalion – 1,000 people.

What are you most proud of?

Business wise, my greatest achievement would be creating the Cobra Beer brand from scratch and against all odds. I turned my student dream into reality – I had begun to dream of creating a less gassy, extra smooth lager that would complement all types of cuisine. It became my mission to brew the finest ever Indian beer and to make it a global beer brand.

Fifteen years later, Cobra Beer is one of the fastest growing beer brands in the UK and is sold in 6,000 restaurants and all the major supermarket chains. In 2003, Cobra beer was awarded two Grand Gold Medals and nine Gold Medals at the 2005 Monde Selection, Brussels. Monde Selection also presented Cobra Beer with the International High Quality Trophy – it was one of only two British brands to achieve this, the other being Johnnie Walker Black, Blue & Gold Label Whiskies. We also launched our new packaging in July 2003, which has already won four awards.

Cobra Beer is indeed well on its way to becoming a global beer brand. It has been exported to more than 35 countries worldwide and we operate international subsidiaries in the US, South Africa and India, with offices in New York, Cape Town and Mumbai. Cobra has been brewed under licence in the UK by Bedford-based Charles Wells brewery and we have now commenced brewing for the worldwide market at one of Europe's leading facilities. Furthermore, we have commenced brewing Cobra in India for the Indian market.

My personal motto is to 'aspire and achieve against all odds, with integrity' and I firmly believe that if you have the passion, drive, attitude and aspiration to succeed, the sky is the limit. I'm just getting started – I'm thrilled with Cobra's current success but I feel the best is yet to come.

What do you consider as your biggest 'failure' and how did you respond to it?

I try not to regret or to have the perspective of having failures – I've made several mistakes and I have tried to learn from them. Starting a beer brand from scratch, there were a number of obstacles to surmount. Instead of wasting my time and energy regretting, I prefer to learn, to look ahead, to improve on the non-successes and build on the successes.

Why do you make 'contribution' to others and to your community an important part of your ethos?

I believe that today increasingly no one can be inward looking, as communities, companies and countries and as individuals, we all have to be outward looking; we all have to reach out and engage.

Cobra embraces the ethos of contributing to others and to the community at large.

This is incorporated in our business principles, which have guided the company since its first day of operations:

- Cobra never asks any of its customers for exclusivity. We firmly believe that the restaurants we supply (our trade customers) should have the flexibility to sell all beers, not just ours, and should offer a variety of products to their customers in turn. Customers should always have a choice.
- The company treats all its customers and suppliers alike as everyone we work with is an extension of our team. It is by working together effectively, responsibly and in an entrepreneurial spirit that we can achieve our mission and live our vision.

- Cobra strongly believes that the company should fulfil its responsibility on all levels and not just growth and profits.
- Community support. Each day, Cobra Beer supports a number of charities, organisations, Asian groups or events, community projects, festivals, sport, student initiatives, arts and entertainment, etc. The charities Cobra Beer supports, to name a few, are The Loomba Trust for the education of children of poor widows in India, The Prince's Trust, the Army Benevolent Fund, MacMillan Cancer Relief, etc. Our team firmly believes that we have a role to play in giving back to the community, be it at a local, national or international level. Myself and a number of Cobra employees are also involved with charitable organisations – not only can we support them with our time and efforts, but we share expertise with them. Personally, I directly support a number of charities and am a patron and trustee of various organisations.
- Continuous training – we believe in lifetime learning. There is training for everyone in the company on a regular basis. Our programmes use a combination of in-house, online and external courses, delivered by our managers, outside suppliers and academic institutions.

With regard to environmental impact, we have implemented a paper recycling programme in our aim to become a paperless office. This concept of waste reduction also operates at the manufacturing level, where Cobra's brewer turns leftover grains into feed for farm animals and our Indian brewer uses wastage from surrounding farmers to generate power and where waste water is treated in an effluent plan and supplied to neighbouring farmers to irrigate their fields.

This ethos of giving back is about not only being the best *in* the world but the best *for* the world.

Do you think higher education and an MBA were critical to your success?

Chartered Accountancy and Law provided me with a solid professional, business and corporate knowledge background that laid a strong foundation for running a business.

As for running a business, although education is by no means essential to being a successful entrepreneur – Bill Gates left Harvard University and Sir Richard Branson did not go to university – I think having an education is not only a fallback but also gives you excellent grounding and confidence and can give you credibility, especially in the early days of starting a business. Attending the Business Growth Programme – a 'mini MBA', tailored to business – at the Cranfield School of Management was a turning point in my career and in my business life.

Who are some of your role models?

My mother's grandfather, Dinshaw Dadabhoy Italia, has always inspired me and I embrace his motto, which was 'to aspire and achieve' to which I added 'against all odds, with integrity'. My mother's family, as a business family, was certainly an influence on me.

My father's family is from a long military line and my father was General Officer Commanding-in-Chief of the Central Indian Army, from the Gurkha regiment. Growing up in the Army, I was instilled with a strong sense of hard work and perseverance, and I truly believe that with these factors, combined with passion and desire to succeed, success is always achievable and the sky is the limit. My father also advised me you have to be not only an efficient team but a happy and efficient team. He advised me to go the extra mile and take initiative: be innovative and creative.

Any advice to young people reading this?

My advice is to never forget the importance of education and to never stop learning. I firmly believe in lifelong learning and in being outward looking.

What is your favourite poem that moves you?

'If' by Rudyard Kipling.

If

If you can keep your head when all about you
Are losing theirs and blaming it on you;
If you can trust yourself when all men doubt you,
But make allowance for their doubting too;
If you can wait and not be tired by waiting,
Or, being lied about, don't deal in lies,
Or, being hated, don't give way to hating,
And yet don't look too good, nor talk too wise;

If you can dream – and not make dreams your master;
If you can think – and not make thoughts your aim;
If you can meet with triumph and disaster
And treat those two imposters just the same;
If you can bear to hear the truth you've spoken
Twisted by knaves to make a trap for fools,
Or watch the things you gave your life to broken,
And stoop and build 'em up with wornout tools;

If you can make one heap of all your winnings
And risk it on one turn of pitch-and-toss,
And lose, and start again at your beginnings
And never breathe a word about your loss;
If you can force your heart and nerve and sinew
To serve your turn long after they are gone,
And so hold on when there is nothing in you
Except the Will which says to them: 'Hold on';

If you can talk with crowds and keep your virtue,
Or walk with kings – nor lose the common touch;
If neither foes nor loving friends can hurt you;
If all men count with you, but none too much;
If you can fill the unforgiving minute
With sixty seconds' worth of distance run –
Yours is the Earth and everything that's in it,
And – which is more – you'll be a Man my son!

Where do you see Cobra developing in the next five years?

Cobra's Grand Canyon plan (named after the fact that I was flying over the Grand Canyon when this plan originated) is to be a $1bn company by 2010.

Karan began his career at Ernst & Young and qualified as a Chartered Accountant in 1986. He graduated in Law from Cambridge University in 1988 and in 1989 he founded Cobra Beer, a premium lager brewed to appeal to ale drinkers and lager drinkers alike, and also to complement food. It took more than five years for the brand to establish itself, but it is now a familiar sight not just in restaurants, but on supermarket and off-licence shelves and in bars, clubs and pubs.

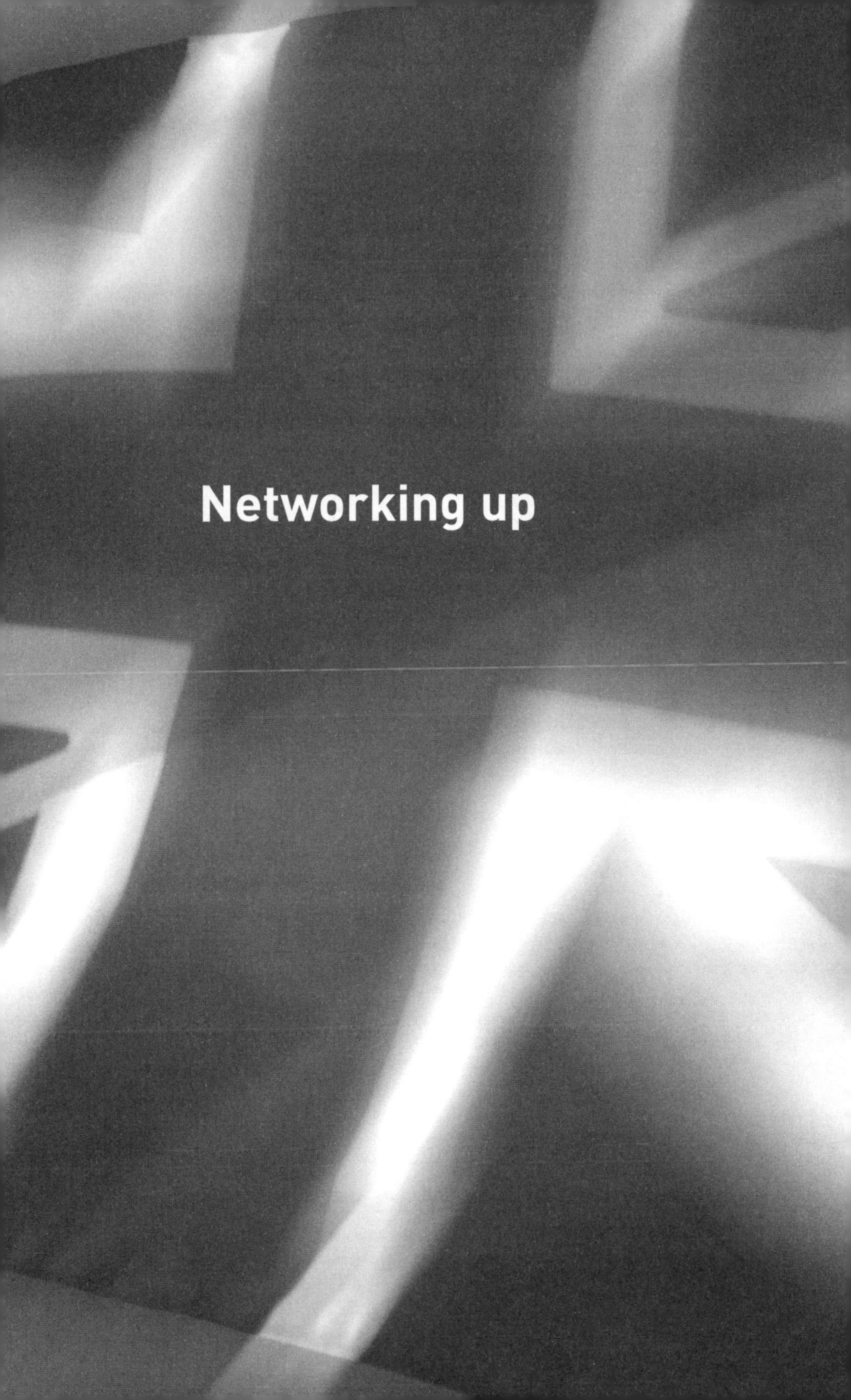

Networking up

An interview with Saundra Glenn

The first thing I noticed when I met Saundra was the energy she carries with her. Perturbed that I was feeling cold she immediately crossed the hotel lobby and shut both doors facing the reception. Saundra is the founder and owner of Kinlock Communications, an event management and PR company specialising in intercultural concepts. She has aided in the design and delivery of several high-profile events including the 'Multicultural Conference on Competitiveness and Enterprise' for EEDA and the University of Luton, 'London Schools and the Black Child' for the Mayor of London and Diane Abbott MP, and 'Recruiting for the 21st Century' for ACFF and the National Black MBA Association. Dynamic, bubbly, full of energy and charisma and yet there is a compassion and genuine appreciation of her personal and cultural history that I could not help but be touched by.

Can you tell me a little about your upbringing and the influence that your parents had on your growth?

My parents both came to England from Jamaica and they met through their religion, as Jehovah's Witnesses. My mother's side of the family were economically stable and for that reason she flew while my father came by ship. Both my parents had high values and we all lived by them (I was the middle of four children). We were raised without television and instead our parents would encourage us to play word or communication games to strengthen our vocabulary. *The Daily Telegraph* rather than the television is where we got our knowledge. My mother was known throughout our neighbourhood and she commanded respect with the elegant way she dressed and communicated with others. She did not have to say anything but she was always treated like an important lady. I learned how to respect myself from my mother's example. My father was a stone mason and he was one of the first members of a professional guild, recognising the importance of having a good name to show your quality. His work was impeccable and he would lay each brick perfectly. Much of his work with the strong foundations will last longer than the people who commissioned it. I learned from my dad that work can be fun as he always enjoyed his work and brought a spirit of fun to what he did.

Did being a Jehovah's Witness shape you?

It remains with you. It is not something that you can just pick up and put down. I remember at school our headmaster was very good at integrating us with the rest of the school. Because we could not attend assembly the headmaster used to plan tasks that we could do. I would not say my culture or religion played as large an influence as it might have with others. When growing up my mum taught us a 'when in Rome do as the Romans' philosophy. In fact, my parents came from the Commonwealth, they listened to the BBC on the radio. When they came to England it was as if they were returning home, coming to the motherland. They felt like this towards England. Although at one point in 1975 my father wanted to return we did not want to go with him. Unfortunately he died in a road accident in 1983 so his wish was never realised.

What were your early goals and ambitions?

From the age of 15 I was clear that I wanted to be a journalist. I was always a fine middle-stream child. I was great at English, an 11 out of 10, but terrible at maths, my worst subject. When I shared my aspirations with my teachers they said I was dreaming beyond my reach. I was told to be realistic and that I could be a nurse or teacher. Anything outside of the norm was a 'no no'. I think that the teachers at the time could not conceive of any pupil going on to something better than their own field of work. After school I went on to Barnfield College where I attained results putting me in the top 4% of the country in my chosen subject. I commuted for many years on the 'BedPan' line as my first job was at EMI in London, followed by a successful career at British Leyland's head office where I worked in the offices of the chairman and company secretary. I believe I'm amongst a small number of African-Caribbean professionals who had access to the kind of education I gained at the hands of the National Enterprise Board members and peers who ran a publicly controlled giant of its kind. At only 21 years of age British Leyland groomed me for an executive career by affording me the opportunity to train towards a full company secretarial career. Privatisation was looming and I left the company when it moved to Uxbridge but often wonder if I had stayed whether I'd have become the Britain's first black company secretary.

After leaving Leyland you chose to go abroad. Why was this?

Before deciding to go abroad I had a stint at Ove Arup (Arup Economics) where I had the joy of being part of the Birmingham Olympic Games Bid for the 1992 hosting. Arup was another great experience and it was a difficult decision whether to leave a nurturing environment where I already had my own junior secretary or accept an opportunity to work in the USA. I took the latter and emigrated to New York as a stenographer for Brook Street Bureau. There was a sense of honour and privilege in the opportunities being presented to me and it motivated my decision to accept them. In addition, my 'real' extended family were spread across the States and my desire to meet them was great. Suburban life at the time meant that as children we used to call many people our cousins, aunts and uncles, but there was no family tie. During my time in the States I met over 90 other Kinlock relatives and a great many more through marriage. I felt a sense of belonging and kinship that had been missing from my life in the UK. Many people think I made the wrong decision by returning to the UK, but ultimately 'home is where the heart is.'

What did you do in the US?

I held many positions with varied work experience. I took depositions using stenography, worked in major law firms, and even learnt to trade soya beans on the stock market at Marubeni. I worked in the offices of Armand Hammer at Occidental Petroleum, and spent a short period at 9 West 57th Street in the offices of Kohlberg, Kravis, Roberts & Co – the kings of mergers and acquisitions. It was at this time that I became greatly influenced by Reginald Lewis, a Harvard-educated black lawyer who also worked out of 9 West and bought Kraft Foods (Beatrice) from KKR. Mr Lewis wrote a major novel, *Why should white guys have all the fun?*, and he pointed out his ethos for business life, revealing that many great deals are concluded on the golf course and over dinner as well as in the boardroom. I enjoyed learning from him. My combined influence of my parent's confidence and poise gave me the ability to fit into the billionaire culture, while at the same time keeping my identity.

What would you say is your identity now?

British black with an African heritage weaved with Jamaican and Scottish! I am British though first and foremost. When I go back to Jamaica, I only have to walk on the street and they can tell I am not from there and I still get charged twice as much by the taxi drivers. I would also say that I have an American persona as some would say that I 'came' into my own while living in New York. That experience changed my aspirations and outlook.

What are you most proud of achieving, personally or professionally?

Coming back to England from the US and being accepted as a mature student on a Masters in Journalism course at the University of Westminster. I had the opportunity to do my dissertation in South Africa looking at the plight of the people in the Kalahari, the indigenous people. The experience in South Africa was very humbling. Professionally I am proud to have received the European Federation of Black Women Owners' Award for Public Relations in 2003. I was also nominated for a Carlton TV Multicultural Award the same year.

What motivates you?

I am motivated by knowing that I am creating change in a small, sometimes invisible, way for the benefit of my community. I am also motivated by the successes of our own UK sprung black 'heroes' and 'sheroes.' There are so many but to name a few I have witnessed the emerging professional roles and careers of Lord Herman Ouseley, Paul Boateng, Baroness Amos, Baroness Howells, Joy Nichols and Yvonne Thompson and this gives me hope for the future of my community of people, and our access to opportunity. Nothing gives me greater pleasure than performing a service to enhance the potential of African Caribbeans, or to share our history to help others to greater awareness of our past achievements and future potential. I am motivated by my personal contribution to our combined successes. I am also a believer in divine intervention.

You call yourself a 'strategic networker'. Can you give us any hints or tips as to daily practices or activities you think are responsible for your success?

I think that in this country, unlike in the States, if you are a success you are looked down upon or resented. I make a conscious effort to reward those who achieve success. For example, when I heard that someone had achieved an important strategic position in government I sent them a bottle of 21-year-old rum and a congratulations card. I normally do this the same day that any good news comes to the press. I think it is important to pay homage to my community of people not only at times when I need their support for a project, but when they least expect it. Their greatness is ignored by the media in large part. It is our own personal duty to make sure that we acknowledge achievements in some form or other.

At conferences I make it a point to speak to the speakers and organisers of an event. I shake their hands and tell them that I am looking forward to meeting them again in the future. I always follow up by e-mail too.

I love not being typically the same as everyone else. My business is driven by my late mother's faith, and the past assistance of family and friends. I have built up over the years an enormous database of suppliers and practitioners and it is my own personal visibility and quality control that have made the company successful. If you are invisible no one can see you.

If you were to give only three keys to networking, what would they be?

1. Prioritise your contacts at events and don't be scared to put yourself in front of people. Look to see who will be useful to you and make sure you meet them. My advice is at every meeting you go to meet at least two contacts and get two business cards from potential customers and partners. Be careful that you do not give your card away freely; think carefully who you would like – cards cost money and it might give the wrong impression if you are too free with your contact.
2. Speak to speakers at events. They often get overlooked by the audience but many of them want to know how their message was received. They are often more interested in meeting the delegates than meeting the other speakers. It is important to meet them early as often they leave after their presentation.
3. Make sure that you follow up on a contact, otherwise it is a dead contact. Don't worry if it is a long time since you met someone, just get in contact. I get e-mails from people who met me 18 years ago – now that's a long time!

What is your favourite poem or piece of literature?

'And Still I Rise' by Maya Angelou. I think that it is very powerful imagery of arising. When I was getting over my mother's passing away a friend used to send me a greeting card monthly with quotes by Maya. I remember one that struck me deeply: 'Above all survive, survive elegantly.'

Where do you get this strength to survive elegantly from?

Firstly from the adoration and admiration of my late mother, Hyacinth Evadnie Glenn (nee Kinlock). Secondly, from all those who have enormous belief in me. I try not to let any of them down. Even people who don't know me well think that I can do great things. It is this belief of others in my potential, in what I can achieve, that drives me. I'm only human but I am not scared to make mistakes or own up to them. Most recognise that I do not settle for humdrum, bog standard, everyday type scenarios. I strive to be unique. To leave a mark. Therefore, I think success comes from a job well done leading to word of mouth recommendations, and from my personal belief in added value. Rather than aiming for 100% I strive for 110 or more. 'Surviving elegantly' should be the only option.

Saundra is the founder/owner of Kinlock Communications, a business consultancy that specialises in a range of intercultural concepts including the A-Z of branding, brochures, exhibitions, PR and event management where 'diversity' is the theme.

The heart and soul of politics

An interview with Ram Gidoomal CBE

Sitting in the Atrium Café, Millbank, Westminster, I am surrounded by journalists and photographers, all watching the news carefully to see what the fate of the BBC will be with the outcome of the Hutton Inquiry. I make my way to the restaurant downstairs to see Ram Gidoomal, successful entrepreneur and businessman, now philanthropist, candidate for Mayor of London and leader of the Christian Democratic Party. The quality that strikes me immediately about Ram is his genuine humility, a rare quality in politics, especially for someone who has achieved so much in the field of commerce too. An active patron of the arts, Ram is currently working to bring together a consortium of investors to launch 'Far Pavillions', a West End play. After campaigning in the last Mayoral elections and securing nearly 100,000 votes, without the big budgets afforded other parties, Ram remains committed to transforming London and bringing the value of 'service' back into politics. Whether he wins the race or not, Ram continues to bring inspiration and transformation to thousands of Londoners.

Can you tell me a little about your upbringing and early influences?

I grew up in Mombasa, Kenya. My father died when I was only six weeks old so my uncle looked after us. He had 7 children of his own so effectively there were 15 of us in the family including my mother, aunt and grandmother. Although a Hindu, I was educated at the local Aga Khan school, which was run by the local Muslim community. The school was broad minded and tolerant, providing a perfect environment for all the children to flourish. I took part actively in many activities, including debating, which I can see now helped to instil in me leadership qualities I would need later. One significant event that I remember is being elected head boy. This was unusual because I was not a Muslim and so became the first non-Muslim to be elected to this role in the school's history. Being educated there taught me the values of appreciation and respect for other religions and cultures, something that is still a need in modern-day Britain.

With your father passing away in your infancy, what would you say was your source of strength?

My uncle. In our family no one had been educated beyond O-level standard but my uncle pushed us all to achieve our highest potential. He had three main qualities that he bred into us by his example.

The first quality was integrity and he was known in Mombasa for his fairness. One example that comes to mind is when a child had won a bicycle at a fairground stall. The owner refused to give him the prize, saying that the child did not win and should go home. My uncle found out about this and went with the child to the stall to challenge the owner. He collected statements from witnesses and soon had the stall owner apologising profusely and giving the young boy his prize. My uncle was always involved in fundraising for charities, a business skill and attribute that I too have picked up. Above all he was trusted and respected as people in the community knew that 'his word was his bond'.

The second quality my uncle had was hard work. He was always giving his very best to support his family and I can never say that he knew what it was to be lazy. He was industrious even by Indian standards. The quality that drove him was *dharma* or 'duty'. He saw work as a way to fulfil his duty to God, as well as to his family and community. It was more of an honour, *izzat*, rather than a burden or sacrifice.

Lastly, the third quality he had was that he was very forward-thinking. He was at this time, before the stock market was popular, trading rupees and shillings and making significant profits. He used telegrams to send and receive market information and he had a very global outlook. When I was still in my childhood and transport poor, my uncle was managing to trade business between East Africa, Japan as well as India. He was a strategic thinker and could see a big picture very early for his time.

You have achieved so much in both industry and in the community. When will you stop achieving? Will you know when you have been successful?

As an individual you come to the point where you know 'enough is enough'. You recognise that in material and spiritual terms you come to the point that you accept what you have. What drives you is not 'more' material and intellectual gain. Issues become bigger than the 'self' and success becomes a state, or condition, rather than a possession or acquisition. The material things that the public recognise as 'trappings of success' are merely the by-products of the condition. The successful person lives for humanity.

I can't tell you exactly what success 'is' but I can tell you what it is not. I received my understanding while visiting a slum in India. A villager said to me, 'You talk about your wealth as GDP (gross domestic product). Here we measure our wealth in gross domestic happiness!' Let me ask you, who was the wealthier or more successful?

Can you describe how you came with nothing to the UK and you entered business, becoming a director of a company turning over £200m a year?

I came into business almost from childhood. Whether at lunch or dinner, conversation would always include the deals my uncle was making and what our plans were. When our family was thrown out of Kenya we lost our home, our trading links and the majority of our wealth and possessions. We came to Britain as refugees. My uncle had enough money to buy a corner shop and that was where I worked when I was 16, doing the finances. Not because I wanted to but because I needed to in order to survive.

After studying Physics at Imperial College, London, I realised that my passion for business was a key driver and that this degree was not going to really help me. I decided to do a Masters in Management Science and Operations and secured a job in the City working as an operations research Analyst at Lloyds Bank International. Eventually the glass ceilings and glass doors frustrated me. I was fortunate that my wife's uncle started a trading business in Geneva and because of my banking background he offered me a job. The business, which dealt with commodities, trading mainly with Nigeria, flourished with the rising price of oil and over the years it grew from a small family business to employing more than 7,000 people in over 15 countries. The businesses were diverse, ranging from aluminium in Nigeria to vineyards in France and tea plantations in India.

Has your cultural identity had an impact on the way you do business?

It has been a great asset. I find that my multiple identities help me cope with the fast-moving changes of modern society. It has made me more robust and adaptable. Change has been part of my life. You can't get much more change than losing all you own and becoming a refugee and starting from the beginning in a new country. It makes me adaptable and confident that in a world of globalisation, no matter where I am in the world, I can cope with most challenges.

This week *The Times* again published its 'Asian Rich List'. Do you think that minority communities place an over-emphasis on gaining material wealth?

No. I think that the media tends to focus on this for its own reasons but those who look after the elderly, their families or serve in the community do not receive any recognition for the time and energy they put into community service. It is the same in wider society too. Many of the things that we do in minority communities keep the fabric of society going. It is still uncommon to see many minority ethnic people putting their elders into nursing homes but cultures and practices are changing. With the rising cost of living, income is important, but the media do tend to exaggerate and give undue focus to wealth.

Why do you think that some minority communities are more disadvantaged than others, for example in education and employment?

There are social and economic reasons which are complex. When the 1991 census was published one sociologist commented that Pakistani and Bangladeshi communities came from predominately rural and agricultural backgrounds where they had less exposure to running businesses or the complexities of business in cities. Other minorities such as the Indians came from urban areas which gave them an advantage, allowing them to build on opportunities more quickly. I am sure that this was one reason but there are many more which would take a whole book to outline.

How can we best support communities which are faring in much worse conditions than others?

Awareness, awareness, awareness. Mentoring is a good way to help others see what opportunities are available to them but ultimately we also need to tackle racism within institutions. I recently did some work for a major military unit, which will remain unnamed, helping them to recruit without racial bias. I sat for four days with the four people who were responsible for recruiting and was given the freedom to be an observer. I could not fault their actual process while conducting the interviews but none of the four was actually 'diversity trained' or aware of cultural needs of some of the applicants. The question is, 'How do you change the system?'

Do you think that minority ethnic people who think that there is no racism in modern Britain are naïve?

Yes. There are glass ceilings still and talent does go unfulfilled. It is industry as well as the victims of discrimination that miss out. Companies need to take more risks and widen their nets. Most of the top employers on their milk rounds still visit the traditional redbrick universities when it is a fact that most minority ethnic students go to newer universities due to social and economic reasons. A good example of recruitment practice is Harvard and Yale universities. They have outreach offices in Harlem and Brooklyn in which they have managed to pick up extremely talented students who would not have considered their institutions based on 'reputation' or lack of role models.

My own story is that I only went to Imperial College as it was a 5p bus ride from our corner shop. Only because the number 49 bus passed by was it feasible for me to travel there. Imagine how proud I was when recently I was appointed a member of the Court and Council of the college. This example shows that not all opportunities are available for everyone to study where they want to, especially those who cannot afford economically or culturally to live away from family because they have an active role to play in the family business.

Why do you think that minority ethnic people are so under-represented in party politics?

I will speak only from a South Asian perspective. Our communities tend to be uninterested in politics. There are very few Asians elected in the Conservative Party. We might have a role model in Lord Dholakia with the Liberal Democrats, but I would say that the under-representation is due mainly to the apathy for party politics in the Asian community. At the time of writing, there is not one Asian in the London, the Welsh or the Scottish Assembly, yet in London there are over 1 million Asians. Not a single major party could find Asians to be placed high enough on their party lists.

I decided to run for the last Mayoral election as an Independent and still secured 4% of the vote. This beat the Green Party, even though I was not given the benefit of a party political broadcast by the BBC. I have been the head of a company of 7,000 employees, employing over 600 people in the UK and yet I was ignored by the media. Would it have been different if I was a Richard Branson and my company was led by a white person? That is for others to speculate. On the strength of my policies I received one of the votes of Simon Jenkins (a columnist for the *Evening Standard* and *The Times*) and in a *New Statesman* poll on 'Fantasy Mayor for London' my policies were voted the best by Londoners. One newspaper commented, that if this election were based on policies alone, Gidoomal would win by a landslide. I have a real passion for London and to serve its people.

What is your greatest achievement to date?

I co-founded the 'Christmas Cracker Project' which raised over £5m for charity over a 7-year period. It managed to mobilise over 50,000 young people all working together to make a difference in the developing world. The project included a different theme each year, from understanding the causes of poverty to exploring the benefits of fair trade. The project was one that I did as a businessman. Often we are told that in order to help charities we need to leave business at the door. This is simply not right – charities as much as any other organisation need sound business acumen; they need people to keep their business hats on. A journalist for *Time* magazine labelled my political stance as 'Pro-business-Social Justice.'

Where did you get this passionate interest for serving the community?

From my uncle who was passionate about serving the community that we were part of. Our employees were from the local community and he was always keen to ensure that their needs were fully met. So I too always wanted the best for my employees. For instance, while involved with the seafood division of the Inlaks Group [*where Ram was UK Group Chief Executive*], I noticed that many companies would shut their factories during the winter period due to the lack of seafood supplies, in particular prawns. This would really affect the pockets of the employees as no work meant that they were short at a time when they needed more disposable income for Christmas expenses. I was aware from my family connections that it was possible to obtain supplies from India during this period. I therefore took a trip to India to source supplies for the winter period so that the factories would be able to run as normal.

On this ten-day trip I wanted to visit some community projects. On the last day of a trip I was taken into the slums of Bombay. It was the biggest slum in South Asia. What I saw moved me and changed my life. There were young women in cages, filth everywhere and people begging with severed limbs, some too sick to move.

On coming back to the UK I gave three months' notice and sold my shares. Although it took three years to fully remove myself from my role in the organisation, from that moment onwards I dedicated my life to social service.

Where do you get the inspiration to have achieved and given so much?

My role model is Jesus in terms of spirituality. As a follower of Christ, my life is spent seeking to practise his teachings. He taught very simply yet powerfully and his teaching and treatment of women and the poor as well as his work towards social justice were revolutionary in his time, as they still are today.

Born in Kenya, Ram is an entrepreneur and former UK Group Chief Executive of the Inlaks Group, a multinational employing 7,000 people worldwide, stepping down in 1992 to concentrate on charitable work and community business projects. Ram was made a CBE in 1998 for services to the Asian Business Community and Race Relations.

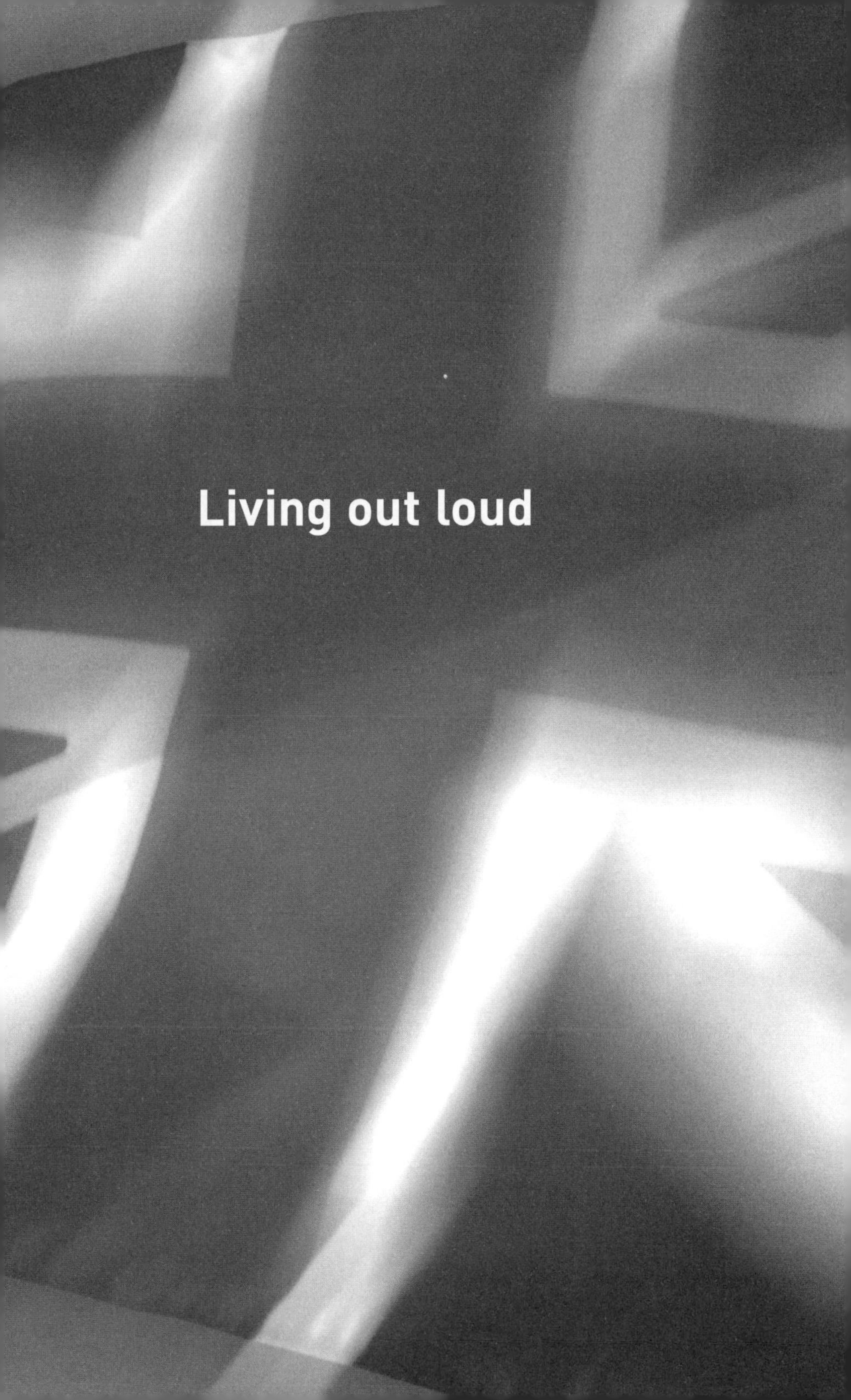

Living out loud

An interview with Angie Le Mar

'What is it like being a black comedian?'

'Very different from when I was white!'

Borough Road, Choice FM studios. Angie Le Mar strides in, having just finished recording for her Saturday morning show. Dressed in a black leather jacket and with sunglasses, she offers me a glass of water and asks whether I want to move to a quieter room. If 'starstruck' was a feeling that could be conveyed without the need for words, it's what I felt sitting with this energetic, powerful and wise woman. Even without doing stand-up comedy Angie's infectious laughter and passion for life move me. You cannot help but leave her wanting to 'live out loud'.

As someone who has achieved 'celebrity', would you say you have also achieved success?

I think of success as peace of mind and good health. It is doing what you want to be doing and living your talent and your gift. When you are young you have dreams; now that I am grown up, success is living those childhood dreams. When I was younger I used to think that success was money, yet when you are around these trappings you realise that the people who have them are just like you or me. Some are horrible too – I don't want to pretend. 'Success' says 'get a fast car', 'designer clothes', a 'big house', yet some of the people who have these so-called successful lifestyles are some of the shallowest and unhappiest people I have ever met. You need to strive for a balance. You can't take your car with you into your bedroom! The real test of peace of mind is that when you are going to sleep, if you feel good then that is real peace. You can have the other things if you want them. I've gone through the bus pass and car being broken down stages too.

What attracted you to comedy? Did you always know that you wanted to do this professionally?

Comedy was an instant gift I always knew I had since I was young. I would pretend to be my mum and dad, when they left the room, in front of my brothers. I would always be standing next to the TV and imagining myself being on the set. My brother told me when I was eight years old that I would be a comedian. I just loved making people laugh and was always good at it.

Can you tell me about your experience of school?

I found being at school very difficult because I was dyslexic. The three words I most hated to hear in the world were 'read this aloud'. I would panic and have nothing to say so I would make people laugh by telling a joke instead. Obviously this did not go down well with the teachers, who threw me out of the class. But the point was that I did not have to read. I would really marvel at those who could stand up and read fluently. I was thrown out of my first school and in my second school I became disruptive again. My parents did not understand why I was having a problem in the school system as in the one subject that I really liked, drama, the teacher loved me and would tell them how great a student I was. I took part in the drama club, school productions, anything that allowed me to express my creativity without reading. To her I was 'Angie the angel', yet in the staff room the other teachers must have been wondering which Angie she was talking about.

Did you go from school straight into comedy?

After I finished school I trained as a social worker at Vauxhall College in South London and did residential social work from the age of 19 to 21. This included overnight reports and the usual paperwork, but in the staff room I would crack jokes and entertain the staff. One day I was meant to be looking after the young people overnight but I sneaked out to do a gig in Lewisham. The young people all stayed in their rooms and said they would support me by behaving that evening – which they did – but I knew that what I had done was wrong and it showed me that I should be spending my time doing what I love – comedy.

Young people receive so many messages about their future careers. How did you distinguish comedy, which is hardly a traditional career, as being right for you?

I distinguished it by the feeling I get when I am happiest. For example, when you think about something all the time, even before you go to bed. Put me in a corporate environment – arrhhh! Put me in an artistic environment and I will thrive. My classroom teacher told me that I would not amount to much, and sure, I was the class clown and the centre of attention. Yet my advice is that if you have a passion you can't doubt yourself, you have to go through things. Just try to stay out of trouble with the law, so you still have options and opportunity. Be rebellious to find your spirit but don't break the law. Find balance in who you are, not in what people want you to be.

How important was your upbringing to your present success?

Very important. We were raised in the Church. My mum and dad had rules for us which were not to be questioned. We had to be in by 9pm every day. It was one way only. Not like the way my son now thinks he can reason and debate with me. I knew that my parents had rules to protect me. They helped me to know what I could and could not do. Rules and parenting are not something that you can rely on the PM to give you. My parents were disciplined in a very loving way, which was consistent. When I stepped through the door, no matter how I had behaved at school, I knew who I was. School is part of a situation but the home is the real deal. The parents have the real control.

My most significant childhood memory, which has come to me on recent reflection as I've been writing my autobiography, is of my dad taking me to drama class every Wednesday and Friday. When people talk about their parents they usually talk about their parents failing them, etc. My experience was the opposite and I am so pleased that my dad was so committed to me. He was always there to pick me up and this gave me a protective feeling. This feeling of protection from men has always been there since I had four brothers and I was the youngest girl. I remember my first fight with a boy on our street and one of my brothers asked me to go back out and fight him. I wanted him to do the fighting for me though!

What are you most proud of?

That I am a mother and a wife. I am satisfied that I make my family laugh and other people laugh and also that I have made a living from doing that. I am Britain's first black female comedian. I started off in small places with a microphone which I would take before the lights were dimmed. I am proud that I could do it, my success has proved that this was my calling.

What has been your most significant life experience to date?

I was sick when I had my last girl. My parents had just gone back to Jamaica so I had no support. I was feeling dizzy and my head was killing. The headaches just seemed to get worse. I went to the doctor and he told me to go straight to King's College Hospital. After examination they thought that I had a brain tumour and they asked me to contact my family immediately. The pace of this occurring was really surreal and it felt like I was in a dream and only imagining this. The fluid on my brain was meant to be at around 15% but it was many times this. The result was that I had to have lumber punctures every week when I was pregnant to drain the fluid down my spine. One nurse did not numb my back properly and I was in absolute agony and could feel the needle go into my back. I was in such pain that I prayed that I did not want to live any more and that God should just take my life now.

At the time I was reading a book called *Conversations with God* so I thought, 'Let me talk to God about this.' I said 'God ... what's the deal? Why have you given me so much talent yet I have to kick down the door to get any work?' The response I got was, 'Your problem is that you keep asking for permission. 'Do you think I am good?' You need to cut out the middle man and go straight to your audience.' I did just that. I decided to start my own company in 2000, Straight to the Audience Productions, to reclaim my power. I came to the point that I gave myself permission to be great, to trust that I knew what I was doing and that the other people I had been asking permission from were probably blagging anyway. I have never looked back. This was the most empowering thing I have ever done for myself.

What was your biggest failure in your career and how did you deal with it?

I was asked to do a documentary for the BBC. I was to go to America for 11 weeks to see if I could make it big there. While I was in New York I was auditioned for parts in the 'Cosby Show' and also 'A Different World'. The BBC insisted that I leave New York to go to LA to fulfil my contract. Although I knew that the opportunity in New York was once in a lifetime, I decided to keep my contract and I flew to LA as requested. When I got there they told me there was not enough 'balance' in the programme and they would not screen it. Unless there was a 'gutter story' – for example, you're always drunk or you are from the ghetto – they were not interested. I got very depressed and I put on 21lbs. Around the same time I was also due to play a part in the sitcom 'Birds of a Feather'. The local newspaper had picked up the story and ran the usual 'local girl makes it big' story. A few weeks afterwards I received a letter from the producer saying they were not able to screen me as I looked too young for the episode. My friends were calling me after the show saying they had not seen me in the programme. I felt very disappointed. I realised I just couldn't deal with the way I was being treated. I had to get out, to change how I dealt with these situations being at the whim of others' decisions.

Who are your role models?

My mum and dad. They believe in karma so they live by their rules and have acted with self-respect throughout their lives. They showed me love and how to love. In entertainment my role model is Whoopi Goldberg. Not many people know that she was a stand-up comedian before she made it big in Hollywood. She has the ability to make very heavy subjects funny. She went into a white-dominated Hollywood as a black woman, dark skinned with long hair and yet she came out with an Oscar. She is also dyslexic and when I found out we have this in common it was 'music to my ears'. I could match this disability to someone I admired. I promoted her when she was writing her book and came to London. I also discovered that we are both left-handed and both Scorpio. I admire Oprah Winfrey too. She just has clean power that comes from beliefs.

Do you have a mentor who has coached you?

Yes, my mentor is Rene Carayol, the broadcaster and business writer. I met him while interviewing him on the radio during his book launch. He talked about the importance of having a mentor so live on the air I asked him whether he would mentor me. Rene asked me the question, 'Where do you want to be in a year's time?' He then helped me focus by asking, 'What am I doing today to make that happen?' If you are making music, you are not going to get there by just continuing to make music. You need to take active steps towards your goals. Every day I can be very busy but it does not mean that I am contributing to my plan. He also taught me to be around like-minded people who support my goals. I value him as a mentor as he is honest and direct – he tells me the truth about what doesn't work.

How do you see yourself contributing to the wider community?

I am part of 'Role Models on Tour' delivering workshops in schools, prisons, youth clubs, to give young people positive role models. To have knowledge is useless if you don't share it. I want to create a drama school, which is affordable and deals with the whole person. It's going to be called the 'Angie Le Mar School of Expressions'. It will be similar to a 'big brother, big sister' organisation. Young people who are excluded from school can come to this school to learn a wide range of the arts – dance, drama, ballet and singing. We will also have training in how to help them write, direct and produce their own work. The school will be starting next year and be based in Lewisham, which is where I am from. Whoopi Goldberg has agreed to be the patron of the school and the Straight to the Audience office will work from there. At the moment I am building a strong team for the project.

Have you any advice for young readers of this interview?

Get to know what you want as opposed to what you think you need. I wanted to be on television but I didn't need to. Put yourself in the environment that shows up the gift that you have, not the gift that you don't. Be honest with yourself and learn to be with your feeling of being uncomfortable but being true to who you are. The more you don't tell people, the more they will hurt you. Respect yourself and clarify what you believe. We are who we are because of our experiences, not in spite of them.

Nothing has to be done before you're 30. When you get to 30 you realise that everything before was just experience to take you to the next thing. The road of life is long and it is important that you enjoy yourself along the way and have peace of mind. Whoopi lives her life like 'this might be it'. In her mind she is already a success. It is developing the attitude that 'I have made it already in this bit of my life', right now. Notice when you have nice moments and enjoy them. It's never too late to do what you want to do and don't delete what you've done so far. Reading *Conversations with God* made me understand that you don't need religion to connect with God. My brother used to say to me, 'what the mind can conceive the man can achieve'. Never be put off by your ambition and big dreams. Some people ask me, 'Why start a school, why not just do a workshop?' I like to think *big* and to go for my dreams rather than think small and live small.

What's next for you?

Movies. I am working on two movies. One is called *There Are Black Folk Here* and the second is a *Waiting to Exhale* type of film. At the moment I am also writing a sitcom called 'Eddie and Angie'. I am working on an autobiography called *Read This Aloud*. I chose this title as these words were my biggest demons, what I most feared. Being dyslexic is my problem but it is a price I have paid. It works for me now.

[I leave the interview with hope. Hope that dreams can be fulfilled . . . that laughter can come after tears . . . and that what hinders us can be used to move us forward and inspire others along too.]

Angie made history with the first sell-out show by a black comedienne in London's West End. She has appeared frequently on TV, most notably in four successful series of Get Up, Stand Up *and the popular* Angie Le Mar Show *airs every Saturday morning on Choice FM. Angie is currently working on a film project based on the Black British experience as well as writing her autobiography.*

The 1% Club

An interview with Janet Soo-Chung

As the CEO of Sheffield South West Primary Care Trust, Janet is responsible for the health care of thousands of patients every day. As one of only 1% of CEOs in the National Health Service from a minority ethnic background, Janet balances her family life with the obligations of her demanding position. As a graduate entrant into the NHS I am encouraged that Janet not only sees her career growing with the NHS but actively works to encourage others to progress and explore the career success that is open to them.

Can you tell me a little about your upbringing? Are there any significant childhood memories that you feel shaped you for the present day?

I am third-generation British-born Chinese, the eldest of four children. We were brought up in a typical three-generation Chinese home; my father's parents lived with us. I was always encouraged to work hard at school and to always do my best, whatever the circumstances.

Being the eldest of four I was always aware of the expectation that I should be responsible and set a good example to my sisters and brother. My parents were self-employed and owned their own business. My memory is of them always working hard and they took few holidays.

What are your early memories of your education? How important was the role of education, both informal and formal, to your success?

I have very happy memories of primary school but I was always aware that I did not share the same background as my classmates. I was fortunate to have several teachers, and a head teacher, who were particularly supportive and kind.

Why did you decide to join the NHS management development programme? Can you describe the programme and what skills you learned?

During my final year at university I began to think through the career choices that were available to me. My degree was in Psychology and for some time I had been keen to pursue a career as a clinical psychologist. I applied for and was accepted onto the programme which was Masters degree level at that time. At the same time I was accepted for a place on the NHS General Management Training scheme. I opted for the latter.

It was a two-year programme which incorporated some academic study and a series of placements working in hospitals, community health services, district and regional headquarters of the local NHS. This gave an excellent overview of the NHS, its services and the issues faced by the service every day – both strategic and operational. I learned that the NHS is a complex organisation, that the many frontline clinicians and other staff need to deliver as teams and that there are always ways in which services can be improved – even where resources are sometimes a constraint.

You decided to leave the graduate programme six months early and apply for your first job. By the age of 29 you were appointed a director and became a chief executive at 35. What are the qualities that helped you rise so quickly and what would you advise others to do who feel stuck in their roles?

Whatever post I have been in, I have always been focused on delivering the goods to the best of my ability. I have always enjoyed my work and been committed to it. I also believe that no matter how much you know, and however much experience you have, you can always learn and develop further. One of my main guiding principles is to work with and through others.

For those who may feel that it's time for them to move on, I would advise them to take the time to pause and reflect on the experience and roles undertaken to date, to think about the things they really enjoy about their current role, and to talk to people working in the careers or jobs they aspire to.

Only a small proportion of senior NHS managers is drawn from black or minority ethnic groups. What specific things has the NHS done to address this and what more do you feel can be done?

Like many other organisations, both public and commercial sector, the NHS has some way to go in building a workforce that is truly diverse. At the present time, from more than 1 million staff, people from black or minority ethnic communities comprise 35% of doctors and dentists, 16% of nurses and 11% of non-medical staff. Fewer than 1% of NHS organisations have a BME chief executive.

The recent initiatives and drive to promote and achieve an ethnically diverse workforce through race equality are led from the front by the chief executive of the NHS, Sir Nigel Crisp, and this is to be welcomed. All NHS chief executives are to take a personal lead and these commitments are backed by a leadership and race equality action plan, a performance framework, mentoring scheme and a national BME forum. There is also a specific programme, 'Breaking Through', targeted at managers from BME backgrounds.

BME staff are not less able or less ambitious than others, but may need encouragement and support to overcome barriers to progression. A barrier to many people working in the NHS is the lack of visible role models. This is important as it can show BME staff that they can aspire to the most senior posts, that it is possible to go further and faster in their own careers. Over the years, I have been approached by many BME staff who have told me how pleased (and surprised) they are to see someone from an ethnic minority background in a senior position.

Mentoring can also be valuable in helping people to identify opportunities, to provide encouragement and support and to increase confidence and understanding. I am currently mentoring someone from within my own organisation and hope that this will be beneficial to them, but I expect to gain from it myself in terms of a greater insight into the issues and constraints faced by many, and playing my part in resolving these.

With so many professional accomplishments, what are you most proud of achieving outside of the work environment? Do you feel that the pressures of being a CEO have prevented you from having active interests outside of work?

Outside of the work environment, I think my 12-year-old son, Christopher, gives me the most pride and pleasure. He has just completed his first year at secondary school and is doing well. He is good at and enjoys sports and has a terrific sense of humour.

Chief executives have many demands on their time and juggling these and maintaining a reasonable work–life balance is a challenge. However, I'm not complaining since I very much enjoy what I do and am fortunate to be working with some very good colleagues who are especially dedicated to health care.

When I'm not at work I enjoy reading and spending as much time as possible with family and friends.

What do you consider to have been the biggest obstacle in your career and how did you respond to it?

I think sometimes the obstacles that we encounter reflect our own attitude and thinking, which can be inflexible or constrained – if only out of habit. Sometimes a lack of confidence can hold us back. I have and will continue to think positively, focusing on what I could gain rather than what I could lose.

Who are the role models who have inspired you?

No one person – I am lucky to have worked with a lot of very good and experienced people, and have learned from their many desirable qualities and skills.

Have you any advice for people reading this book who want to enter the profession?

The NHS is the largest provider of public services and the largest employer in the UK with 1.3 million staff. It is a hugely complex organisation with, in my opinion, the most important role of all – helping people to stay well and treating those who are ill or have been injured. I would encourage all people to think about the NHS as a career option – there are many areas of work available. Local colleges and universities will be able to give details of the kinds of training available. Many hospitals and community health facilities hold open days to enable people to see services and these could be useful sources of information and advice.

What is next for Janet Soo-Chung? Where do you see your focus in the next few years?

I have been in my present post at Sheffield South West PCT for about 16 months now and there is still work to be done here.

The NHS has just published its Improvement Plan, which will guide our work over the next few years. I have just completed building the senior team here at the Trust and will be looking forward to working with them to continue developing our services to patients.

Janet has worked in the NHS since 1983 in a number of senior management posts. She got her first director's post at the age of 29 and was appointed to her first Chief Executive post at 35.

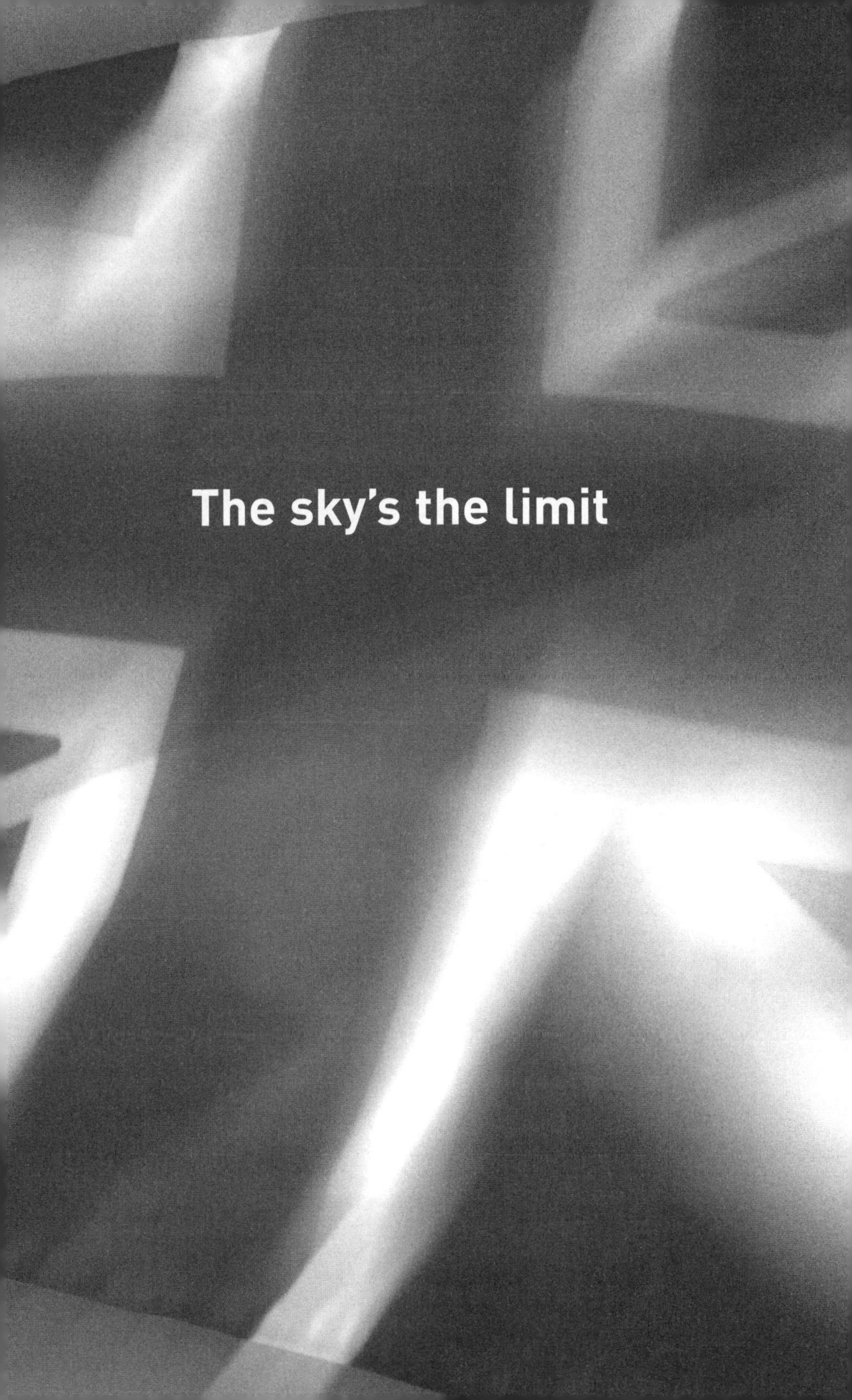

The sky's the limit

An interview with Mohan Ahad, 'Rocket Man'

Few of us have not marvelled at images of rockets being launched into space. It is not merely the launch that is significant but rather its meaning, humankind 'transcending the known' and moving into the vaster unknown. This can be both exhilarating and frightening at the same time. I met Mohan at a conference at Luton University. A week later he was in Nice where investors were vying to be involved in his company, Microlaunch, which develops the miniaturisation of technology that will allow small organisations to build and launch small satellites. His personal journey is as inspiring as his company.

Can you tell me a little about your upbringing and early influences?

It is difficult for me to recall my very early memories. Significantly for me my mother was diagnosed as paranoid schizophrenic when I was only six years old and she suffered from severe depression. Mental illness in society is considered a taboo to discuss but in our local community it was even more of a taboo. People in our community would view mental illness as a curse and so there was very little support. Social services at the time didn't know how to deal with the problem and we felt shunned. My response to this was to become a social introvert. I would spend most of my time reading a lot of fantasy and sci-fi and also comics like Asterix and Tintin.

Given your mother's medical condition, how did this influence your early choices?

My father didn't insist that we go straight into work. He recognised that education was very important and he liked to brag about our education to others. He himself was a very intelligent man, teaching himself English before he came over to this country. He was very active in the local mosque, in the Labour Party and also assisting the local Bangladeshi community with issues regarding immigration and basic problems such as visas and settling into this country. My parents did not so much influence my career aspirations; I always knew what I wanted. From the age of 13 to 14 I knew it was to build rockets as that's all I had the passion for. I tell people, 'the only reason I was put on earth was to get off it!'

What are you most proud of?

I am proud of setting up Microlaunch. It is entirely different and changing things. I will be proud when we have a successful launch in two years' time but the real test of my success is when others follow my example and say, 'I can do this myself'.

What is success?

To realise you can be yourself. It is extremely liberating to know you can be yourself and do what you like to do. I am successful but I am not there completely yet.

What do you consider your biggest failure and how did you overcome it?

The first time I set up a company was when I was doing my MBA. One person on the team thought he wanted to be the managing director. I thought 'hang on' as I also wanted to play a leadership role. Unfortunately he had all the contacts and he wanted to take over. This was very depressing for me at the time and I thought of dropping out of the company and I refused to give him my shares. For two years I did other things and the company fell apart because the team fell apart. Depressed, I decided to move to Leicester. Although I still knew I wanted to run a company I took a few low-paid jobs.

Was an MBA critical to your success?

Absolutely critical. I used to work at DERA (Defence Evaluation Research Agency), I was becoming depressed at my job, my father had passed away and I was feeling suicidal. My friend Asrar sat me down and said, 'Mohan, what do you really want to do?' I told him that I wanted to build rockets. He told me that I had an idea on paper but I needed to understand how to get money and I needed a career. He suggested an MBA would be the best way for me to do this. Although the MBA was critical, when you start a company you learn skills that you cannot get simply from studying. The key skill is entrepreneurship but I find as the saying goes, 'the harder I work, the luckier I get'.

You seem to be very confident and outgoing for a person who was highly introvert. What brought around this change in you?

Before I was confident I used to listen more to others' opinions this made me depressed. The transition I have undergone has been a gradual process. I have used a lot of self-examination therapy which has helped me to open up. The first thing was to admit to having a problem. Mental illness has always been a huge factor in my life. I have discovered that what's really important in life is not money. First, it is to 'be yourself'. Second, I have learned that good things as well as bad things happen. Third, what stops me giving up is that so many people believe in me.

You were involved in the Cambridge Summer School. Can you tell me more about that?

Yes, there were 50 of us and it took place over one week. While there I met Alan Barrell, Entrepreneur in Residence, who introduced me to Candace Johnson [*co-founder of Astra Satellite, now part of SES Global, the world's largest satellite operator*]. Attending the Summer School helped everything take off. Shai Vyakarnam, the course director, became a partner. It gave me the confidence that I had someone else who believed in me. I have learned it is crucial to have the support of someone who is very respected who believes in you. A good many entrepreneurs don't believe in themselves and so they find it hard to influence others. It was important for me to get across to people that I am not a mad rocket scientist!

How do you ensure that you connect with people?

Don't judge people on their job function. Avoid putting labels on people and instead find out what they enjoy. Start connecting with 'What would *you* like to do?' I get support from my family; we have had a traumatic time. I also get support from my team.

What motivates you?

My dreams. A dream is something you aim for but never achieve, for example a society that is open or freedom from everyone else.

What are your hobbies and interests?

Cinema, watching DVDs and speed dating. A problem that I have as an entrepreneur is that I can't switch off.

If I were to meet you in five years, can you describe yourself?

I should be long retired. For me my work is fun and play. I am an entrepreneur but I don't want people to remember me. I would rather have people go on to do great things for themselves. I want to be the smallest achiever.

Born in Luton, Mohan is a chartered engineer with a degree in Aeronautics and Astronautics and a Postgraduate Diploma in Satellite Communications Engineering. He worked for several years for the Ministry of Defence and DERA testing military aircraft systems, before studying for an MBA. He has now founded his own company, Microlaunch Systems, which aims to develop a new space rocket to place microsatellites into orbit for aerial photography, telecoms, scientific and other purposes.

Keeping London safe

An interview with Assistant Commissioner for London, Tarique Ghaffur

Sitting in my lounge by 'The Castle', in Green Lanes, North London, I sip my cold coffee while reading over the Sunday papers. Suddenly the portrait of a police officer catches my eye as I notice that he is going to be honoured with a CBE. As I read on I learn that he had overcome an internal inquiry which was dropped to be promoted as one of the most senior minority ethnic officers in the MPS – the Assistant Police Commissioner for London. His story and obvious commitment to policing inspired me and I knew that I wanted to feature him in the book. As he is extremely busy I never got to meet him but he was keen to support this project. I guess the point is that you might not get to meet all the people who inspire you, but they can still make a difference for you and others.

Why did you decide to become a policeman? Were your parents supportive of this career choice?

I became a policeman, initially, through necessity. Along with my family I had been kicked out of Uganda by Idi Amin and we were penniless. I wanted a new beginning and the police paid relatively well at the time. My parents were initially wary about this decision and were obviously concerned about how an Asian officer would be treated. Later I think it is fair to say they were very proud of my achievements.

Can you remember your first posting? How were you received as an Asian officer on the beat by your local community and work colleagues?

I was posted from training school to Salford. The reaction of people varied across the board. When I arrived at my first police station they didn't believe I was a police officer. Despite my warrant card they rang the training school to confirm I was who I was claiming to be. Many in the community were really interested, as they hadn't seen an Asian officer before. Once they got to know me their reaction was much more welcoming and many in the community were really pleased to see a young man from a different community serving in Manchester.

Your rise within the ranks has been inspirational. Why do you think there are so few minority ethnic senior police officers and what do you consider are the most effective ways to remedy this?

There are many reasons why there are so few senior police officers from minority ethnic backgrounds. Whilst minority communities are much better represented as being successful in many of the more traditional professions and in business, there is clearly under-representation within public life. There are very few minority senior civil servants or chief executives of health authorities around. Things are changing and we are seeing many more minority ethnic officers joining the Met. These record numbers, however, will take too long to filter through the traditional promotion structure. Direct entry, a recent proposal from the government, may go some way to bringing in people from different communities at higher levels of the police commensurate with their abilities. In terms of positive action I think we need to be much more daring. I am not in favour of affirmative action, such as that seen in the USA; I think this can be divisive. That said, there is a great deal more we can do to encourage officers to go for promotion and we could be significantly more innovative in positive action initiatives. In traditional 'conservative' institutions such as the police service this is always a great challenge but one that I believe is starting to have support at the highest levels.

What was the most challenging situation in your career to date? How did you respond to it?

As a newly promoted sergeant in Moss Side after the disturbances in 1982. I was brought in by the then chief constable, James Anderton, to head a robbery squad. Through hard work and working with the community we significantly reduced street crime over the period to such an extent that James Anderton remembered this in a letter he wrote to me after my recent award of the CBE.

What are you most proud of achieving in your career to date? Why did you choose this moment?

I was awarded the CBE in the Queen's birthday honours 2004. This was a very proud day and recognised and rewarded me professionally. It also served to thank my family for the many days away from them as well as those in the community who have been such ardent supporters throughout my career.

Throughout your career you have been a role model figure to a lot of individuals through your achievements, writing and championing of policing. Who are your main role models?

Nelson Mandela is probably my main role model. His dignity through adversity and his elevation to an international statesman was awe inspiring. His role in the truth and conciliation process was a period in world history that is particularly poignant to me.

What advice would you give to people considering a career within the police service? What qualities do you see as essential for their success?

My first advice would be to join. It is a great career that offers such variety that no two days are ever the same. The pay is good and you will make many friends. Professionally it is challenging and you are at the forefront of trying to make a difference to people's lives. Be yourself would be my main advice. We need a police service representative of a great world city, from all walks of life and backgrounds.

What is your vision for policing in 21st-century Britain and what is next for you on your career path?

My goal is to help the new commissioner make London the safest major capital city in the world. My current post, which includes leading world-renowned units such as the flying squad, homicide and child protection teams, allows me to be right at the front end of improving the lot of Londoners. It is something I love doing and with the communities I work with we have a chance of making tomorrow a better day than today.

After starting his police career in 1974, Tarique is, as Assistant Commissioner with the Metropolitan Police, the highest-ranking Asian police officer in the UK. In 2004, Tarique was awarded a CBE for services to policing.

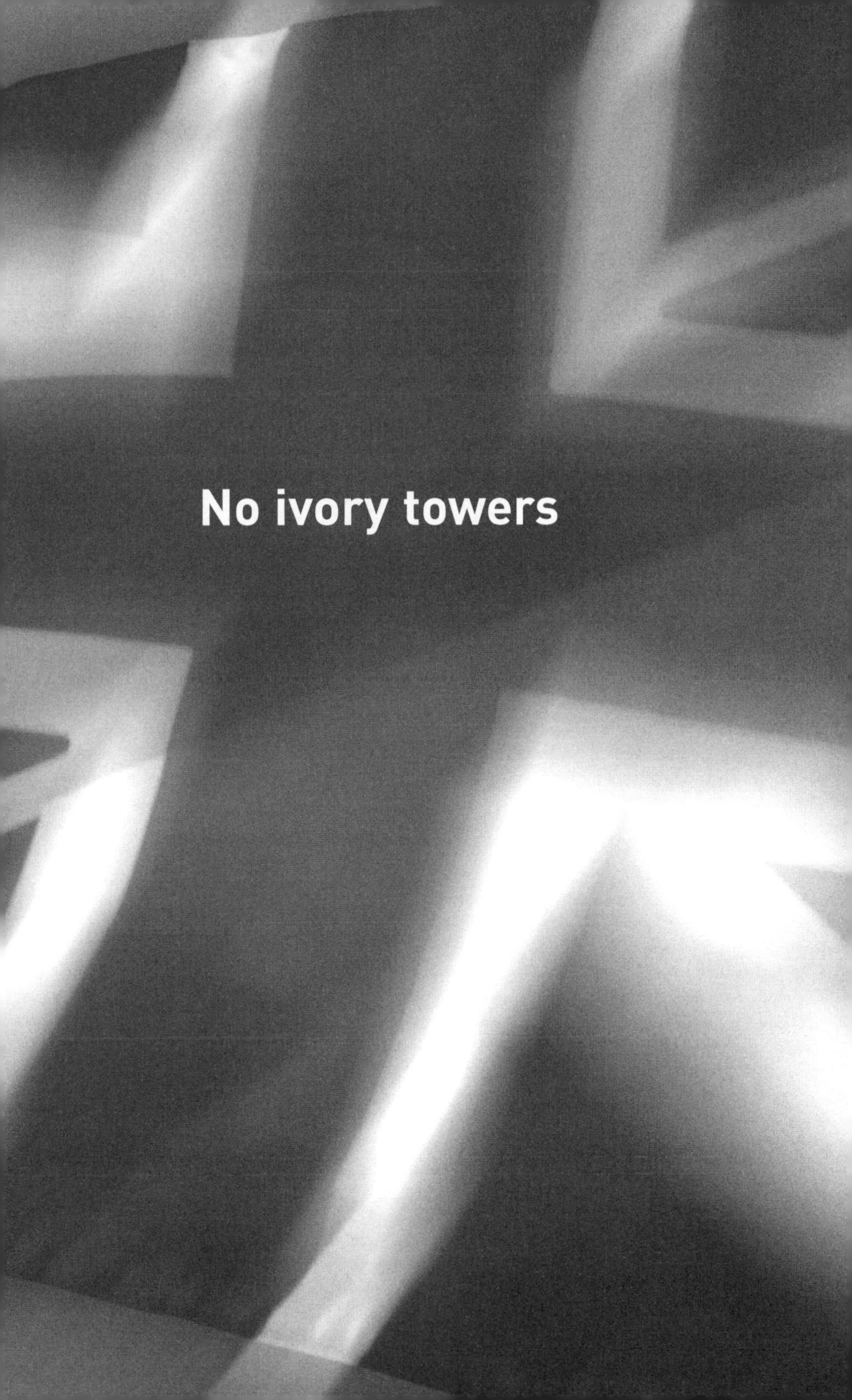

No ivory towers

An interview with David Adjaye

Walking through Hoxton, East London, I am filled with the sense of regeneration. Of an area surrounded by council blocks that is re-inventing itself as one of the most fashionable places to be 'seen' in London. I wait for David in his offices, watching his staff, all dressed in casual jeans, field telephone calls and work over their plans. The atmosphere is energised. 'David is going to be late,' I am told, 'he is always running late.' I get the impression that David is a man who gets 100 things done, and all before breakfast. An architect who has within five years grown a practice to beat several high-profile studios, he meets me after his 'working' lunch.

Can you describe where you were born and what early memories from childhood stand out?

Having to negotiate different cultures as my family moved around, and realising the differences.

Were you aware of your cultural identity as a child and how did this impact upon you?

Yes, I come from a proud Ghanian family and this has given me a lot of confidence.

What inspired you to become an architect? When did you know this was a profession you wanted to train in?

There was no specific event that triggered me off. I really didn't know what architecture was till I was 18. Just being alert and aware of space stimulated me. I was quite reflective as a child and lived under tables till I was ten. I didn't play too much with other kids. My brother has a physical and mental illness and I was aware of all the limits that were imposed upon him due to the construction of space in everyday architecture. I was fortunate to have a truly global upbringing and I grew up in many cultures, Christian and Muslim. These helped widen my understanding of cultural impact on space.

When I was 18 it was my art teacher, Mr Jenkins, who is now in Finchley, North London, who inspired me. He was totally encouraging and understanding of my lack of specificity about what I wanted to do. He knew however that I had a strong interest in space and art and he encouraged me to pursue that by going on to do an Art Foundation course.

What was your experience of the education process?

I feel that I crafted my own tailor-made education. I did my degree in one year although it normally takes three years. I got a job in an architectural office after finishing my art foundation. I knew then that this was the career that I wanted to do. I applied to all the schools in the UK but all of them said that I needed to start a degree at the beginning even though I had work experience. A man named Stan Sherrington at South Bank University gave me a chance to go straight to the third year. He was very instrumental for me. I graduated with a first class honours degree.

How did you first make the transition from working for others to starting your own practice?

It was the height of the recession when I graduated so there was not that much work. I knew that if I worked for someone else I would simply be in the background. I had been in Japan for the last year of my MA and so I came back from there inspired and motivated. The Head of School at South Bank offered me a teaching job at the school. I took the opportunity and started my own practice from my bedroom, which eventually expanded to the living room, the garage and then an office.

What makes your practice different?

We have a different voice. For us architecture is a creative discipline. It is a voice that expresses my cultural identity and incorporates my experience in Africa, Asia as well as Europe.

Why do you think there are so few prominent minority ethnic architects?

I think it is very sad. The problem starts with the very word 'architect' – it is a European word. Space and the concept of space on the other hand can be found in all cultures.

Immigrants have always found it difficult in the West, however a lot have achieved financial success in the late part of the 20th century and we have seen the rise of a professional immigrant class.

The civil rights bill in the US only took place in the 60s so one can argue that it is only possible now to become a prominent figure because of the work that our forefathers did.

It's not easy being a public figure in the press. Yet I know it is of value to others. I didn't have a role model when I was young but had to search for one. Now I get many calls from people whose sons and daughters are interested in architecture. It comes with the territory.

So do you have role models now?

I admire a lot of people but the person who has had the most impact on my life is my mother. She is my greatest role model. Both my mother and my father chose a different life for their children when they left their villages in Ghana and decided to be pan-African.

How do you describe yourself, culturally?

I am interested in the idea of not suppressing my identity as an African British male. I like to express my creativity through the references I have made. I am very interested in world cultures. I don't feed from one direction and pretend to be something that I am not.

What is your definition of success?

Being able to do that which you love as your job.

What do you consider to be the biggest failure or disappointment in your life and how did you respond to it?

I don't qualify experiences as best or biggest or last . . . disappointment is an ongoing lesson and it teaches you the rich tapestry of life.

Adjaye Associates recently won the contract to design the Nobel Peace Centre in Oslo. How do you view this piece of work?

There has never been a centre for the Nobel Peace prize. It was a donated building which we will turn into a Peace Centre. It will celebrate the 100 Laureates who have won the prize and will be used for future ceremonies. We aim to finish it for June 2005.

Have you any advice for readers aspiring to a career in architecture?

Don't be afraid of dreaming. Go for your ambitions. Aim high and don't be too surprised when you get there.

What is the next move for Adjaye Associates?

We are aiming to grow an international presence and work extensively in America, Norway, Spain, Africa and become an international company.

Born in Tanzania and a graduate of the Royal College of Art, David is recognised as one of the leading architects of his generation in the UK. His studio Adjaye Associates is currently engaged in the designs of the Nobel Peace centre and the new home for the Museum of Contemporary Art in Denver. David has also just presented Building Africa, *a documentary on the architecture of the continent, for the BBC.*

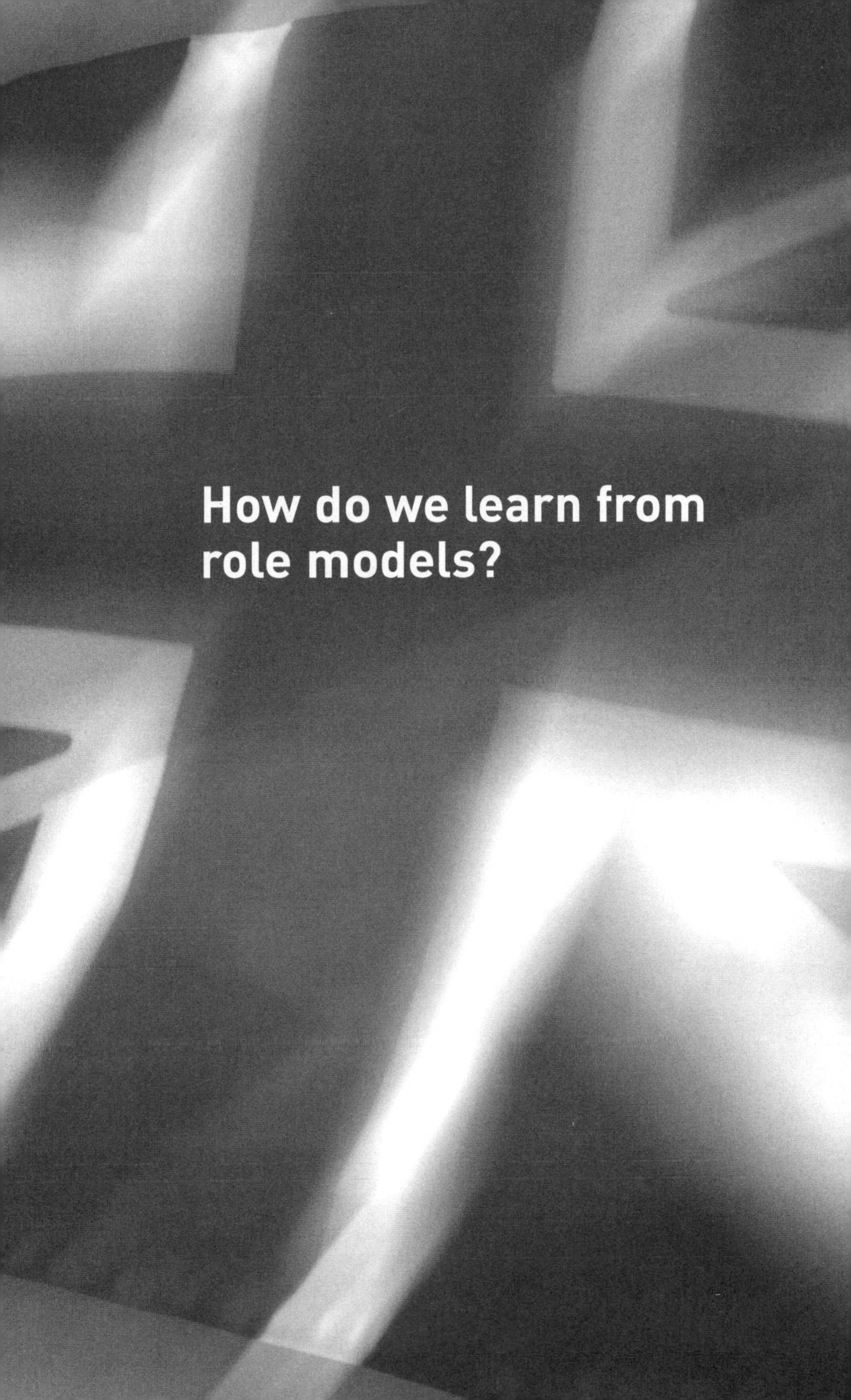

How do we learn from role models?

There is a variety of ways to learn from role models, even if you can't meet them in person. Below are a few ideas. Try them out to see which ones work for you and what results you get. You can use them in any context and apply them to your situation.

Learn to model

By modelling I don't mean walking up and down a catwalk or painting small figurines!

Modelling is the ability to replicate excellence in yourself

Modelling is taking what you find brilliant and useful in another person's behaviour and recreating it in yourself. What do I mean by this? Let's take an example. How many light bulbs have you made yourself recently? Obviously none (unless you happen to work at a light bulb factory). You don't need to make any yourself when you can buy a light bulb someone has already made. *They have done all the hard work* in developing and manufacturing the bulb so all you have to do is flick a switch and bingo, the light bulb works.

You do not need to learn from scratch how to do things someone else can already do well

All you do need to do is to discover *how* they do what they do well and then duplicate it. If they can do something well, *so can you.*

How do I model how other people do things?

We all know people who have great talents and are really good at things, including *you*. For example, my friend Kishor is good at pool, Katie is good at art and Marcus is good at drinking (orange juice of course). I'm sure you can think of talented friends.

Yet when you ask them how do they do what they do, what makes them so good, it is likely that very few of them can articulate, let alone tell you *how* they do what they do well. More often they will reply with 'I dunno, I just do it!'. This is true, as often they don't know how they do what they do or can't break it down and explain it.

Modelling is an easy procedure with simple techniques. If you follow these steps and put them into practice you will get the same results as those you model.

Step 1: Choose your company wisely

As a child we learn most of our behaviour from those around us – usually parents, siblings, relatives, teachers and friends. Over time we develop similar habits or traits to those people who are closest to us. For example, we might use similar phrases when happy or angry. We might like what they like and dislike what they dislike. As humans we are always affected by our environment to some extent.

We tend to become like the company we keep

Now you can use this simple fact to your advantage. Simply:

Associate with those whom *you want* to be like or who possess qualities that *you* would *like* to develop in yourself

We're not saying that you should give up your friends but rather look to see whether the friendship brings out things you want in your life or things you don't any more. It is great to have friends who we relax with and have fun, this is *very important.* Yet we also need friends who *motivate, inspire* us and are *excellent* at what they do, getting *great results* in the area we wish to develop.

Step 2: Find a mentor

For every area that you want to develop in your life, whether it's your studies, your fitness or your career, find a mentor.

Mentoring is a formal relationship in which an individual, normally someone who has achieved personal success in their field, is prepared to meet someone on a regular basis to help them develop their goals. For example, a music industry executive might mentor an aspiring record producer or a mother who is good with numbers might mentor someone in maths and science skills. The role of the mentor is to act as a guide to help you get the most from your abilities and to steer you with advice if you should want it.

There are many mentoring organisations, several are detailed in the Resources section, that will help connect you with somebody suitable. Before you contact them you might ask yourself the following questions:

1. What skills would I want to learn from a mentor?
2. How regularly would I want to meet a mentor?
3. How would I know that this mentor is right for me?
4. At the end of the mentoring relationship where would I like to be in my life?

It's important you also look around you for mentors. The mentor might be somebody you know through work or study, perhaps a colleague of your dad or mum, maybe a teacher. Try to get to know them if you don't already. If they are unwilling to help, obnoxious or arrogant, leave them and find someone else who is really good at that subject. Generally you will find that people are approachable and are willing to help.

Everybody likes to be listened to attentively and appreciated. Find someone good at your subject, listen well, and they will enjoy sharing their ideas with you

At this point I will stress that if you use people you are likely to not learn much as the relationship will fail. If someone does give you their help, be a friend to them in return, outside of study, and share what you can give to them. Give to them when you want nothing in return. This method is not about copying someone's homework or work project, or being two-faced to gain knowledge, rather you must try to develop a friendship based on mutual giving. If you sincerely want to learn from somebody, they can see this and will usually be willing to give you some help.

When you have a mentor, notice carefully the complete behaviour of the model you have chosen. Let's take an example of a student you want to model because they are really good at a subject:

Do they make notes in class or at work? What type of notes? Or do they just listen?

What do they do in between sessions? What books do/don't they read?

Why do they find the subject interesting? Do they talk about it?

How do they talk about their ability to do the subject/to understand it?

How do they study the subject? When do they study?

What questions do they ask?

Observe observe observe observe observe observe

After you have observed your model, *do exactly as they do.* Ask yourself, 'How can I do what they do now?'. Duplicate it and try it out for yourself. For example if you find that John who is really good at history tends to pull articles from a particular journal, try reading it yourself. If John believes history is interesting, ask him why. Try to develop the same level of interest in history that John has. If you do everything you can that John does well, soon you will be getting the same results. Wait and see!

Step 3: Act as if

One of the most effective ways to learn from a role model, whether you know them personally or through books or the Internet, is to literally 'try on their behaviour'. There was a recent TV series called 'Faking It' when ordinary members of the public had to convince others that they were experts in subjects they knew nothing about before the programme. One person had to convince people he was a F1 driver while another had to persuade an audience that he was the conductor of an orchestra. One of the main lessons of the programme was that the individuals had to take on the characteristics of the role – literally to 'be' the person they had to be in all aspects. This would involve taking on the physical posture of the person, being aware of how they would stand, greet others, developing the verbal skills and vocabulary that would be expected of someone in that role.

It's a similar story to actors who are asked to play demanding parts. Some of the most well-known actors take the time to literally experience what life would have been like for their characters. An actor who plays a doctor might volunteer or observe those in an accident and emergency ward. A person who plays a homeless character might spend time in a shelter. Eventually the actor even takes on the mindset of the character so that they think in the way the character would – actions consistent with the character follow automatically as a result.

What if you don't have access to a mentor or can't find someone whom you really feel cuts it for you and has something to teach you? One of the things you can do is explore books, the library and the Internet to read about the lives of people who inspire you. There are many great websites in the Resources section that profile inspirational people, especially people from BME backgrounds. The value of these websites and books is that they are much more available than a personal mentor might be.

You might ask yourself the following questions:

1. What about this person's life is similar to mine?
2. What are the most important lessons that I can learn from this person?
3. How can I practically apply these lessons to my own daily life?

It is important to remember that not everything about another person will apply to you. Each of us is unique but we can all learn something from each other. When we learn about someone we have the potential to develop the qualities that they have in our own lives. Look at the qualities that the person has and see whether you have these qualities in you. If not, how might you develop them? If so, how might you strengthen them?

Throughout history there are examples of talented people whom sadly we can't make use of directly. For example, we cannot stroll into a room to ask Einstein about physics or call Da Vinci on the telephone for inspiration or creative ideas (unless of course we happen to have a time machine and my names Bill and your name's Ted!). But even if we can't do this, we can still learn from people who are no longer alive or whom we will never meet.

We can learn anything from anybody using the subconscious mind

How? A simple but very powerful technique is to take on the character of the person you wish to model. If you are an actor or a drama student you will know that the best way to play a person is to become them, at least while you need their resources, behaviour and skills. This technique has been used throughout history by geniuses from many fields. For example, it is reported that Walt Disney always insisted on doing the voiceover for Mickey Mouse and would become so animated they modelled his hand movements and gestures for the cartoon character. General Patton is said to have thought himself to be the reincarnation of great past generals. He was said to have an uncanny genius for applying successfully traditional medieval warfare techniques to modern-day mechanical warfare situations.

There was a Soviet psychiatrist, Dr Vladimir Raikov, who used hypnosis to get his clients to identify closely with figures from the past. One client who modelled Rembrandt was able to paint so well that when she came out of hypnosis she did not believe she had actually produced the artwork. We are not asking you to go into a trance, but just try these simple techniques below and see how they affect your performance.

There are three main ways you can use the 'act as if' principle to do well at studies:

1. Select someone who is really good at something you want to develop or knows about the subject. They can be from history, fiction or fact. Let's imagine you are studying Stuart history at A-level and are looking at the English civil war. Rather than model a historian who understands the subject, in this case it would be helpful to understand the situation better from one of the principal characters. So you might choose Cromwell, Bishop Laud or King Charles.

   First get as many books and resources as possible on the person you are to model. Read and observe information about their character, their clothes, behaviour and mannerisms. When you feel you know enough about the character, I want you to imagine them standing in front of you. Then step into the character's body and try to perceive the world through their eyes. What would the character be feeling, seeing, hearing, thinking about the situation they are in? Just observe how you are thinking about the situation. Use as many senses as possible. How would they talk? Walk? Address others? What are your impressions? Now give a speech or explain the answer to a question you have been given from the perspective of your character.

   You can then step out of the body and record what you have observed. Literally when you do this properly your whole perspective will change. Perhaps you can sit an exam or solve a problem while enjoying the perspective of Einstein or Aristotle!

   Other people vary this technique by simply asking themselves the question, 'What would my role model do?' You might have seen people who wear wrist bands with the inscription 'WWJD', which stands for 'What would Jesus do?'. Others might have 'Buddha' or another personal guide. The wrist band is a good idea to keep thoughts focused and to practise 'remembering to remember' your own role model. You might have nothing written on your wrist band but it being there serves as a reminder to you.

2. Another technique is to form an imaginary council of advisers whom you can consult on different issues. For example, you could have a council member for each of your subjects. For maths problems, perhaps you could have the famous mathematician Bertrand Russell advising you. For history perhaps the English historian Elton. Take the time to imagine a room where all the council members have a meeting with you:

   Where are you seated? What are you wearing?

   What is the room like? What shape is the table?

   What are your members wearing? What are they saying to each other?

   You can then ask each member of the council to give you advice about a question you have. Listen carefully and record the answer given by the subject. Don't worry if you feel that you are just making it up: keep on going and just imagine what they would say if they were talking to you.

   The more you use your imagination, the better results you will have. Although the process might seem unusual, the insights you will receive will surprise you.

   You can use the above technique to ask advice from anybody. Why not make Richard Branson your finance adviser or Arnold Schwarzenegger your personal fitness coach? Perhaps you might choose some of the role models in this book as your advisors? Just play with it and notice the *results* that follow.

3. If you are too embarrassed to step into the perspective of a great figure, or to have a council of advisers, a simple step is

to imagine you are already good at the thing you want to be good at.

You already have *all* the skills and resources you need

Let's imagine you wanted to be confident about your studies. Just imagine you are *now.*

How would you be acting now if you were confident?

How would you be feeling? How would you be talking to yourself and others?

How would you walk around, sit and stand?

What are you doing differently now that you are confident?

Just take the time to imagine yourself behaving like this and doing what you want to do successfully. Again use all your senses. Then do what you want to do confidently, as if you are, and just notice the results.

There is a saying: 'If we cannot think our way into a new way of acting, we can act our way into a new way of thinking.' The key to this is consistency and taking a playful attitude in trying this on.

Step 4: Be a role model yourself

The ultimate message of this book is that you are a role model and by fully developing your talent you have something to share with others – a unique contribution.

There is an old Rabbinic story of a rabbi called Zusia. The great Hasidic Rav Zusia was dying and all his students were gathered around him, praying and crying. Then Zusia began to cry and one of his students said, 'Rav Zusia, why are you crying? You have lived a righteous life, you have raised up students, and you will be received into the world to come.' Rav Zusia answered, 'I am crying because now I understand that God will not ask me, 'Why were you not Abraham, or why were you not Moses?' God will ask me, 'Why were you not Zusia?' And I will not know what to say.'

It might be your family or a friend who looks to you, but to somebody you make a lot of difference. 'To the world you may be just an individual, but to an individual you may be the world.' We can look at the role models in this book to see what we can learn from them, but we also need to look at our own gifts and to be brave enough to acknowledge and share them.

Each of the role models and people you admire is a mirror, an opportunity to look at yourself. The Talmud, a Jewish mystical text, says: 'We see things as *we* are, not as *they* are.' There is a story of a traveller who comes to the top of a mountain and there is a city below. He asks an old man sitting there, 'Tell me, what are the people in the city down there like?' The old man asks him, 'How were the people in the place you just came from?' The traveller replies, 'They were awful, spiteful and jealous people.' The old man responds, 'That's the same as the people down there in this city.' The traveller, relieved to get this information, goes on, using a different route, cursing to himself. A few hours later another traveller comes by the top of the mountain and asks the old man the same question, but when the old man asks him what the people were like in the town he just came from he replies, 'They are friendly, generous and great people to be with'. The old man responds, 'That's the same as the people down in the city below.' The young man, grateful, makes his way down and spends many happy days.

The message of the story is that our experiences often tell us more about ourselves than about the thing in itself. This includes what you notice. For example, if you have a friend who is good at building up people around them, ask yourself, 'How do I support others around me?' If you look you will see that you also have qualities that are similar to that person's, even though the means of achieving the result might be different.

There is a beautiful quote by Marianne Williamson (in *A Return to Love*) which was quoted by Nelson Mandela when he was inaugurated as President of South Africa in 1984. Although often quoted in books its message for those of all faiths and none is clear.

> *'Our deepest fear is not that we are inadequate. Our deepest fear is that we are powerful beyond measure. It is our light, not our darkness, that most frightens us. We ask ourselves, who am I to be brilliant, gorgeous, talented, fabulous? Actually, who are you not to be? You are a child of God. Your playing small doesn't serve the world. There's nothing enlightened about shrinking so that other people won't feel insecure around you ... We were born to make manifest the glory of God that is within us. It's not just in some of us; it's in everyone. And as we let our own light shine, we unconsciously give other people permission to do the same. As we're liberated from our own fear, our presence automatically liberates others.'*

You are better at some things than other people will be. Even if we think we are really bad at something there are always people who have more difficulty. If you are really good, *share what you know with others*. This might be explaining something or giving some ideas for improvement. Or simply encouraging them and supporting the other person.

You cannot give anything in life without receiving back in proportion to what you give

Sure, maybe this cannot be proven scientifically, but consider this: just by teaching something you have to learn it well for yourself.

Teaching something to others is the best way to learn anything for yourself

If we are genuinely interested in helping someone else, without being condescending, arrogant or derisive, they will almost always be genuinely eager to assist you should you need it in the future. A secret worth more than anything in this book is:

Successful relationships are the key to doing well at your studies, in work, in life

It stands to reason that the more good friends you have, the greater variety of talent you are around, the more resources you will have available should you need it. Remove yourself from little cliques. Try to meet as many people from different groups, departments, fields and subjects as you can. Make it your business to make as many friends as possible whom you genuinely like. You will find that not only will your social life be great but as you are there to help others, there will be someone there for you. Try it.

Finally achieve your own dreams

What do you want?

Your aspirations might be different from those of the people in this book. Whether you want to improve from a D grade to a C, or whether you want to become a straight A student; whether you want to get promoted or become the best manager in your company, what's important is that you look at what you want.

One of the common characteristics of those who made the biggest difference in society is that they take on big problems, not complain about small ones, such as the bus not being on time. Martin Luther King Jr's problem was the struggle against apartheid. Gandhi's problem was English occupation of India. The question is, do you have big enough problems that are worthy of your life?

There is a beautiful quote by George Bernard Shaw called 'Splendid Torch'. He writes:

> *This is the true joy in life, the being used for a purpose recognised by yourself as a mighty one; the being a force of nature instead of a feverish, selfish little clod of ailments and grievances complaining that the world will not devote itself to making you happy.*
>
> *I am of the opinion that my life belongs to the whole community, and as long as I live it is my privilege to do for it whatever I can.*
>
> *I want to be thoroughly used up when I die, for the harder I work the more I live. I rejoice in life for its own sake. Life is no 'brief candle' for me. It is a sort of splendid torch which I have got hold of for the moment, and I want to make it burn as brightly as possible before handing it on to future generations.*

When you read the interviews in this book you might ask yourself, 'What is my dream that I want to pursue?' There is a saying that we stand on the shoulders of giants. Be more aware of role models around you, not only in the media, not only in obvious places. Look to learn from others and also be a role model yourself. Yes, you have something to teach others.

Ultimately role models are noted for how they act, not only for what they say. We hope that you find your role models and you go on to inspire many people by making your dreams into reality.

> *'We must be the change we wish to see in the world.'*
>
> Gandhi

Inside the role model

> *Role models chosen carefully have the power to widen horizons and open up possibility.* Guardian *columnist, Gary Younge comments: 'Employed subtly and judiciously, role models present us with route maps by which we can begin to contemplate not only possible directions in life but also, more importantly, how we might get from where we are to where we would like to be. By exposing us to our potential, they can be empowering.'* *The Guardian* 27 March 2002

Having looked at the individual stories of people who undoubtedly are role models, it's interesting to look at what exactly makes a person qualify as a role model. It is a very personal question. I (Steven) remember first exploring this issue several years ago with a room full of teenagers who had been expelled from mainstream schooling, in a special education centre in Camden Town. I had been asked to do a workshop on self-esteem and goals and I wanted to start it by looking at who the class admired. I asked them, 'Who do you consider successful and who would you like to be like?' Answers ranged from Richard Branson for his wealth to Tupac Shakur for his music.

When the question was changed slightly to 'Who do you admire who has made the biggest impact on you?', what was interesting was that many of the answers were people such as parents, mum, dad, gran, friends, uncles. The people who most struck them were not removed and inaccessible but people they related to perhaps on a daily basis. It was the teacher who cared for them or showed trust, the parent or step-parent who supported them day in day out, perhaps the friend they felt was a talented singer or gifted musician, or they admired the way somebody could solve difficult maths problems.

So although initially it was role models from the mass media, suddenly it turned to people who perhaps made them tea, listened to them, kept their promise. Ordinary people who make an extraordinary impact. The Business in the Community guide 'Keep on Moving' comments: 'Young people increasingly turn to the media to find role models, but it is important for them to be aware that they are surrounded by positive role models in their daily lives. Members of their family, the woman who runs the local shop, their youth worker, doctor, nurse or teacher – all of these people can be positive role models in their own right; they all have their own achievements which contribute positively to society.'

It was interesting that qualities rather than possessions were admired. Character rather than achievements. A part of being a role model is having qualities that people admire. The list is endless. Let's take an example – what qualities do people look for in a leader? Depending on who I asked I might get answers as varied as integrity, control, firmness, honesty or controlling, direct and commanding. Qualities as wide as the different styles of leadership there are and the different situations they are required to lead in.

The same goes for role models. Rarely do we look to one person for every quality and there is a danger when we do expect perfection from one individual. When we place a person on a pedestal they have no place to go but down. Patrick recalls listening to a famous lady on a radio chat show about ten years ago, explaining what success meant to her. It was all about wealth, cars, houses and big jobs. She said that she hoped many would follow these examples and experiences in her life. Patrick called the radio station and gave his example of success and how people in the most unusual life circumstances can inspire and be role models without even realising. The example he gave was of someone who had recovered from mental and physical illness using amazing willpower and self-belief. For him this was a greater example of success and I can see how this person could be a role model for many, even those not suffering from illness. In this book you will have read the De Gales' interview. Daniel and his family are an example of this – they are clearly role models and I believe their achievement is one of the greatest demonstrated in this book. They will inspire many from all walks of life.

Ram Gidoomal in *The UK Maharajahs*, a book which examines the success of the South Asian community in the UK, points to the role of family and the extended family as providing a context for role modelling. He writes: 'Asian society, with its extended family basis and its emphasis on certain basic values, is a natural environment for role models to be sought and imitated by younger generations.'

He shares an example of his son Ravi who at the time was looking to make a cassette to launch his band. By following the example of his father on a similar project Ravi was able to reduce the costs significantly and contact members of the family to offer their services free or at discount. Ram comments: 'I didn't teach him how to do it, he's learned as I learned, from fathers and uncles and others. Listening to them talk, seeing what they did, observing who was willing to lend money, who could be of help in business. Entrepreneurism is often caught, not taught; and the extended family, the key unit of South Asian life, is a proven incubator of business success.'

Although Ram's comments on the role of the family are fair, not everyone has the benefits of an extended family to learn from. But we might have friends and people close to us whom perhaps we can look to.

Perhaps most important is Patrick's observation that he never used the term 'role model' to describe himself until he realised that people consistently referred to him by that title. But still he rarely uses that term even now. It is a term used by others to describe people who are a model in some way to them. You can't make yourself a role model to others – others choose you. Role models are appointed to this position irrespective of whether they want it or not. Role models are classified as role models based on how others see them. They are appointed by others, sometimes without realising it. Like Patrick, few role models refer to themselves by that title; in fact often they feel uncomfortable when it is used to describe them.

What do role models have in common?

Role models show us what is important to us and what is possible for us. If we have role models who are honest, there is something about that quality of honesty that we admire and recognise in the other person that we have.

Role models rarely take no for an answer. People admire them because they never give up; they will always find a way. Partha Dey describes some of the most important factors to his success: he never gives in; he always tries to find solutions to problems. From his interview you know that he wasn't short of problems. When Patrick was younger, his mother always told him he was stubborn and would question why he never just accepted her point of view.

Role models usually have their own role models, people whom they have looked to for years, people whom they fashion themselves against. More often than not the real role models are brothers and sisters. I believe that we usually choose family or people whom we are very close to because it is easier for us to see the links and building blocks. We can see how they achieved their success.

When you read the interview with Asif Kisson he talks about how he was interested in the natural colours of the chicken feathers given to his family. This is one of the early building blocks in Asif's life that inspires me. From two chickens to award-winning designer, with many building blocks along the way.

When I look at most of the people interviewed further in this book, most quote close family as their real role models. Others say they have no real role models but go on to mention a number of people who have been instrumental in their development.

Role models are often the underdog who achieves the unexpected; they produce a positive result against the odds, especially when others believe they won't. People are attracted to these characteristics.

Role models like to prove people wrong. Partha Dey just keeps going, he sticks to it until he gets there. This characteristic is especially prevalent in the music industry – some of the biggest hip-hop and rap stars persevered and never gave in. The young people who see these stars as role models are copying them; they believe that with perseverance they will one day be Tupac. If only we could transfer some of this enthusiasm to mainstream life.

Most role models have experienced significant failure at some stage in their life. For Patrick, it was during all of his schooling in the UK. In his interview Sir Bill Morris states that his biggest failure was in not communicating the way he would have liked to with his dying wife. This really reminds us that people are looking for role models to be real and down to earth. Sir Bill could have quoted his biggest failure as relating to his professional life. Being a role model is about the person and their rounded characteristics, not necessarily what they do professionally. Some of the most successful people are hardly positive role models. It is more than what you achieve, it is about how you achieve it and the various trappings relating to character and personality.

Role models have personal qualities that make them admired. They are not just admired for their skills, ability and experience in a given field, but also for their personal values such as respect, integrity, trust and honesty all the time in both private and public life. People don't buy cars simply because they look good, they will check out all the specifications or characteristics of the car. If the specifications don't match the looks, they are less likely to buy it. It's the same for role models – people will only buy a consistent role model, the inside must be consistent with the outside, the private and public life should meet the same standard for which that individual is admired.

Role models must be consistent, otherwise people will be confused and question their status as a role model.

Good role models are usually proud of their past and will usually talk about the experiences that helped make them who they are today.

Role models don't have to be wealthy. You can be poor or of moderate means and still be a great role model. Believe in and be proud of yourself, warts and all. Importantly you must accept the warts; you should learn to understand who you are and every aspect of your make-up. Accepting the warts will be evident in your behaviour. Admirers don't expect role models to be perfect; they are actually OK with seeing the warts. It makes it easier for them to emulate their role models because they too will have warts. If people find out that you are not what you purport to be, it calls the title 'role model' into question.

Role models tell the whole story. It is not good enough for role models to talk about where they are in life without talking about how they got there, including all the building blocks and how these blocks link together. If role models try to hide certain building blocks (parts of their life/experience), it will show up in how people view them. There will be something missing or some element of inconsistency in their story. When you read Sir Ram Gidoomal's interview you get a real feel for the man and where he is coming from. He really puts the meaning of being a role model into perspective. I am impressed by Sir Ram when he says: 'What drives you is not more material and intellectual gain. Issues become bigger than self and success becomes a state or condition, rather than a possession or acquisition. The material things that the public recognise as trappings of success are merely the by-products of the condition. The successful person lives for humanity.'

What's it like to be a role model? A model comparison

One of the ways is to compare a role model to a fashion model. This is not saying that fashion models cannot be role models – they can – but it's a useful analogy. Unlike fashion models, who seem to be perfect in make-up and often blemish-free, most role models will have some story of struggle in their life, a history which is not all that comfortable or attractive to talk about. They all have warts in their life and character. These warts help to make them who they are. Back to the building bricks again. There is nothing glamorous about being a role model. The glamour is usually in the minds of those who see you as a role model.

Whereas fashion models are on the catwalk only during a fashion show, role models are on the catwalk day and night and in all circumstances. People will be admiring their role models even when they are not aware. Fashion models can see an adoring audience lining either side of that catwalk. Sometimes role models don't even know the extent of how they are admired by others; they may not even realise they are a role model. Role models must be true to who they are, they must be themselves. Fashion models will strut their stuff walking down the catwalk, but as they leave the stage and are out of sight they can revert to type.

Good role models will always give their time to support and encourage others. I believe that role models will have at least one person whom they mentor and encourage on a personal basis. Why do they do it? Because they remember where they came from and want to give something back. Throughout the interviews you have read you will see these great examples of role models often give back to their communities in a significant way. Karan Bilimoria, chief executive of Cobra Beer, has built an ethos for his company around contributing to others and his community. Again Sir Ram Gidoomal is a great example of someone who supports and gives back – he cites his greatest achievement as raising £5m for charity.

Role models don't normally just wake up and say, let me start doing some voluntary or community work. There is usually a driver emanating from aspects of their life which steers them down this path. Of all the characteristics of a role model I believe this is possibly the one which will be common to most. People are attracted to other people who do ordinary things, we all like people who help, they seem more real and touchable. The late Mother Theresa, when asked whether one needed to do great things to make a difference, is reported to have said: 'It is not necessary to do great things, do small things with great love.'

Role models will help to transfer hip-hop thrills to tip-top skills

Young black boys are especially stereotyped with the music and sports tag. However, when I listen to some of today's teenagers perform hip-hop, ragga and other creative poetic tunes, I am truly amazed. I still wonder how they manage to speak so fast. When these kids start to randomly create hip-hop lyrics without any practice, I am even more amazed by how they manage to think so fast and put together such strong lyrics. They are able to copy their role models, 50 Cent, Tupac and others almost instantly as a new tune arrives; they simply want to be like their role models, sometimes including all the trapping of guns, drugs and gangs. I always wonder how they are able to so easily replicate the style and life of many of their role models. So for these young people the concept of role models really works. The challenge now is to find ways of transferring the desire to copy people who can often be negative role models to copying positive role models. The challenge is to transfer hip-hop thrills to tip-top skills.

The dangers of role models

Having explored the positive aspects of role modelling we should also explore whether there are any dangers to having role models. It's a valid question as often those who are identified as role models shy away from the term. Let's look briefly at some possible concerns and reasons why.

Tokenism

One of the most obvious dangers is tokenism. We see in British society many positive action initiatives. While not as strong as the affirmative action that goes on in the US, it sets people apart from others due to the virtue of their difference. The people in this book are from BME communities, not as tokens but to redress the balance and show that successful individuals from these communities exist as well as majority role models. It is important to note that none of these people represents or speaks for their communities from choice but they do so through the perception of others. Often, as I mentioned earlier, BME people, like all other minority groups, are put under unfair burdens representing more than just themselves.

It is a sad fact that often bias and prejudice come from contact with individuals, not groups. A person might be the victim of crime from a 'white person' and then assume that all white people are criminals. The absurdity of the generalisation is lost in the individual's perceived experience. By highlighting role models from BME communities it is not saying that they are the peaks in the valleys, rather it is saying they are only a small example of the mountain ranges that we are all a part of.

Alienation

It is important that role models are not seen only as individuals who have become alienated from their cultures and communities in their pursuit of 'success'. All the role models in this book were chosen because they see themselves firmly as part of their communities and, more importantly, they want to contribute to their community. Some do this by speaking in schools, while others sit as governors or supporters of community groups and charities. None of them has denied their background.

Avoidance of real barriers

Role models must not be used in isolation and as a reason to avoid addressing other problems that cause people to not fulfil their potential. Because some people have achieved their goals it does not follow that there are no barriers that others will face in reaching for their own. It is not an excuse for government, our educational system, our organisations and each of us to look at whether there is unfair disadvantage to any groups in society. Role models often show what can be done in the face of adversity but it does not mean that the adversity has a positive effect on everyone who encounters it. Many people are treated unfairly, denied educational or work opportunities and face real barriers that we all need to address individually as well as collectively.

The appendix of this book contains a chapter which gives a little more information on the barriers that are faced by BME groups and puts the reasons that we wrote this book in a wider context.

And finally . . .

We hope this book has contained at least one story (and hopefully many more) that has inspired you and that you could see lessons in the lives of others that apply to your life. More importantly that you can see which 'bricks' you need to build your own foundations.

We hope we have shown you that role modelling is something that we can all have access to regardless of our differences and that we all can make a difference in our own lives and to wider society. Role models are everywhere, we just need to consciously choose them.

Role models we have seen are not strangers but often the people right on our doorstep, the people closest to us. It is not heroic things they do that make a difference but it could be the small steps that make the biggest impact on people's lives.

There is a story, I heard, of a young man walking one morning towards a beach. It is twilight and in the distance he sees an old man with a red bucket on the shore, appearing to be putting things into the sea. As he gets nearer to the man he notices that the whole of the beach is covered in starfish that have been washed ashore and the old man is collecting them and taking them one by one into the sea before the sun rises fully.

The young man is astounded. He says to the old man, 'Why on earth are you putting the starfish back into the sea? There are hundreds here . . . there's no way that you can save them all. How foolish.' The old man smiles kindly, picks up a starfish in his hands and gently places it back into the sea. 'It made a difference to that one, didn't it?'

Everything you do, no matter how small, has the potential to have a positive impact on others. Ultimately we would like to leave you a question. It's not 'Are you willing to be a role model?' but rather 'Are you willing to acknowledge *you are* a role model?'

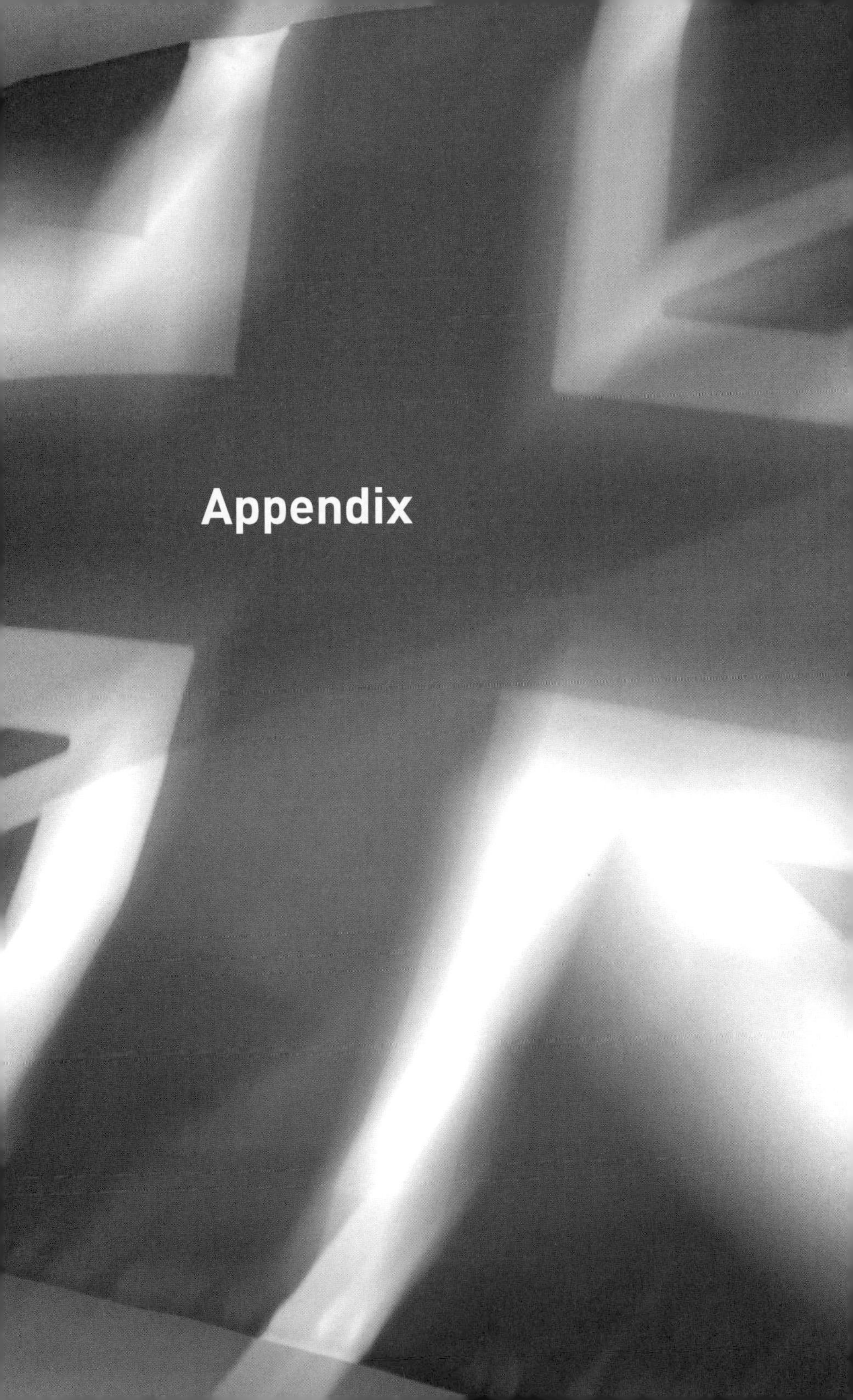

Appendix

'There is no black in the Union Jack'

I (Steven) would be reminded of this on the school coach. It was said in crass humour but I couldn't argue with the fact. So does being visibly different and from a minority community really have an impact?

I live in London. It's one of the most diverse cities in the world. At the time of writing, it is recorded that over 307 languages are spoken in London alone and according to the European Union, London is the most linguistically diverse city in the world. According to the 2001 UK census, at least 8% of Britain's population are from minority ethnic communities. Indians are the largest minority group, followed by Pakistani, Black Caribbean and Black African communities. The Bangladeshi and Chinese communities are the smallest groups. In other words, nearly 1 in 10 of Britons are from minority ethnic groups.

We live in a Britain where the majority of minority ethnic people living here were born in this country and the UK is a place they call home. Some people are second- and even third-generation, with long-established links here. By this I mean that for some their grandparents came to Britain and even their parents were born in Britain – this really is the only home they know. Minority is the majority in at least some London boroughs and also in cities such as Leicester, which incidentally has the largest Indian population in the world outside of

India. Fish and chips has been replaced by curry as the nation's favourite dish, *Bend it Like Beckham* is a hit film and Punjabi MC has made the Top 10.

It's 2005, everyone is treated equally. Britain is multi-cultural and fair. Isn't it?

One of the consequences of being born in this country is that I don't have the experience that my parents had to know where we are now and what exactly has changed – and, more importantly, what hasn't. A little over 40 years ago in Britain, notices could be found in newsagents advertising rooms to rent with caveats saying 'Irish men, wogs and niggers need not apply'. In 1976 the UK government passed the Race Relations Act. This made it unlawful for anyone, individuals or companies, to discriminate on the grounds of race in access to education, training and employment and also the provision of goods and services. But 30-plus years on, how much has changed?

In 2002, one of Britain's most respected polling research companies, ICM, did a major survey to gather attitudes to race in modern Britain. In the survey, over half of the British public who responded said they believed Britain was a racist society, but half also believed that Britain had become more tolerant over the last decade. The report also examined perceptions of racism in education and employment. Interestingly, almost one-third of Black (black and Asian) respondents said they had faced discrimination at school, college or university, compared with 1% of white people. A similar proportion (nearly 33%) of black and Asian respondents said they also faced discrimination at work. This compares with only 3% of those who are white.

Whereas 28% of whites thought colour affected how individuals are treated in education, 48% of blacks and 42% of Asians believed it did. When it came to work, half of the black and Asian respondents believed that their colour made a difference in the way they were treated, compared with one-third of whites.

Very high numbers if we think that problems don't exist.

One of the most disturbing results from the survey was that one-third of black and Asian respondents thought they had lost a job because of racial discrimination.

Perhaps the most interesting question, especially in the context of the 2005 pre-election politicking on immigration, is the responses to the question, 'Has immigration benefited or damaged British society over the past 50 years?' Almost half (47%) of whites thought it had damaged society. This was more than double the amount of those who felt the same from BME communities.

The BBC-commissioned ICM survey clearly showed that tensions and divisions are believed to exist still, but perception can be very different from facts. Perhaps these people *believed* they were treated differently, but come on, it's in their imagination, isn't it? What is shocking is that the actual experience of BME individuals seems to validate the perceptions in the poll results. There are marked disadvantages within minority communities, some significantly more disadvantaged than the others.

Let's look briefly at just two of the areas vital to living and participating in society.

Education

When Tony Blair came to power in 1997 everyone remembered his mantra 'Education, education, education'. Although attainment of all pupils has improved since then, proportionately those from BME communities have not seen the same results.

According to the Office of National Statistics (ONS), Chinese pupils are more likely to get five or more GCSEs at grades A*–C (or equivalent) than any other ethnic group, and 70% of Indian girls and 58% of Indian boys did so in 2002. This success contrasts sharply with the attainment of Black Caribbean pupils. Only 23% of Black Caribbean boys and 38% of Black Caribbean girls achieved five or more A*–C grade GCSEs. Pupils from the other Black, Black African and Pakistani groups had the next lowest levels of attainment.

See Table 1 below showing data from the ONS.

Table 1 Proportion of boys and girls aged 16 who achieved five or more GCSEs (grade A*–C), published 12 December 2002

England and Wales	Percentages
Indian girls	66
White girls	55
Indian boys	54
Black girls	46
White boys	45
Other groups girls	44
Other groups boys	40
Pakistani/Bangladeshi girls	37
Black boys	31
Pakistani/Bangladeshi boys	22

In 2000/1, black pupils were more likely than children from any other ethnic group to be permanently excluded from schools in England. This is an interesting fact given that black pupils enter compulsory schooling as one of the highest achieving groups but leave at 16 being the group least likely to achieve five high-grade GCSEs.

Linda Appiah (MD for Access Educational Consultancy) argues that African Caribbean boys' low attainment coupled with high exclusion rates is an issue in need of serious attention as there is a strong correlation between school exclusions and criminal activity. Minority ethnic people account for 21% of the UK male prison population. Black men represent most of this figure despite making up less than 1% of the UK population.

In higher education, according to the ONS, in 2001/2 people from the Black Caribbean, other Black, Pakistani and Bangladeshi groups were less likely than White British people to have degrees (or equivalent). Among men, Black Caribbeans were the least likely to have degrees (8%). Among women, Pakistanis/Bangladeshis were the least likely group to have degrees (7%). The White Irish, Chinese and Indian groups were among those most likely to have degrees, but they also had fairly high proportions with no qualifications (19% of White Irish, 18% of Indians and 20% of Chinese). This compared with 16% of the White British group having no qualifications. Pakistanis and Bangladeshis were the most likely to be unqualified. Nearly half (48%) of Bangladeshi women and 40% of Bangladeshi men had no qualifications. Among Pakistanis, 40% of women and 28% of men had no qualifications.

The ONS data concludes that despite some ethnic groups being more likely than the white population to have a degree, they were also the more likely to have no qualifications at all or to underperform. In the further education sector, according to the report 'Challenging Racism: Further Education Leading the Way' (2002), all groups of minority ethnic learners have lower levels of achievement than white students. In 1998–1999, whilst 72% of white students completing courses gained a qualification, only 61% of Black African students, 62% of Black Caribbean students, 64.8% of Bangladeshi students, 64.2% of Pakistani students, 67.7% of Chinese students and 68.9% of Indian students completing courses gained a qualification.

Why should we even care about this issue? Apart from the obvious, there are other reasons that it matters to all of us: in Britain, BME communities, with a growing population, will provide more labour which will be critical to sustain the British economy in the future. Within this decade, according to the Labour Force Survey (LFS), 2001–2002, BME communities (not including new migrants) are projected to account for over half the growth of Britain's working-age population. The impact if these communities fail to develop their full educational attainment will affect everyone. Who is going to pay for your pension, be your doctor, banker or lawyer, never mind shopkeeper or taxi driver?

> *'If any individual is denied the opportunity to fulfil their potential because of their racial, ethnic, class or gendered status it is now widely understood that society as a whole bears a social and economic cost by being deprived of the fruits of their enterprise, energy and imagination.'*
>
> Gilborn and Mirza 'Educational Inequality: Mapping Race, Class and Gender', London: Ofsted, 2000.

Employment and income

If BME people do make a successful transition into the workforce, the ONS Labour Force Survey on Employment (2001–2002) shows that in employment as well as education there are marked differences between different ethnic groups.

Whereas men and women from white groups were more likely to be economically active than their counterparts in minority ethnic groups, Bangladeshis had the lowest economic activity rates among both men (69%) and women (22%). Pakistani women also had very low economic rates at 28%. In unemployment, all those from minority ethnic groups had higher unemployment rates than white people, both men and women. According to the report, Bangladeshi men had the highest unemployment rate at 20% – four times that for white men. For all the other minority ethnic groups, unemployment rates were between two and three times higher than those for white men. Interestingly, age was also a factor and from all ethnic groups unemployment was much higher among those aged under 25 than for older people. Over 40% of young Bangladeshi men were unemployed.

The survey shows that young Black African men, Pakistanis, Black Caribbean and those belonging to the mixed group had very high unemployment rates ranging between 25% and 31%. The comparable unemployment rate for young white men was 12%. Women showed a similar picture to men. Bangladeshi women had the highest unemployment rate at 24%, six times greater than that of white women (4%).

The situation was no better for graduates. According to the Cabinet Office Report 'Ethnic Minorities and the Labour Force' (2001), BME undergraduates are still two to three times more likely to be unemployed than their white counterparts six months after graduation with the same level of experience and qualifications.

A test by a London radio station in 2004 sent identical CVs with a foreign-sounding name and an English-sounding name. In no cases did the CV with the foreign name get progressed while the English name did. Yes, we have moved on a long way since the Race Relations Act 1976.

Snowy Peaks

In 2003 Trevor Phillips, Chairman of the Commission for Racial Equality (CRE), gave a speech in which he described how government organisations, although represented at the lower levels with BME staff, became more 'male, pale and stale' the higher one went.

Of the top FTSE 100 companies in Britain, only 1% have a minority ethnic member on the board. Although the NHS has over 40% of its workforce drawn from minority communities, only 1% of chief executives of NHS trusts are from a minority community. Similar statistics can be given across industries.

Organisations are slowly realising that in order to be competitive they need to be representative of the communities they serve and that this can be a business advantage. This has seen a rise in diversity professionals and companies recognising that being diverse is not simply a good thing to do but makes business sense.

In the UK alone, the spending power of those from BME communities is £45bn. African Caribbean men are estimated to spend the most on fast-moving consumer goods. Companies that have specifically targeted staff from minority communities have seen huge dividends. For example, Lloyds TSB saw a 30% rise in profits by making sure their branch staff reflected the community and like HSBC have even developed products that meet communities' religious needs.

Although this is changing on the bottom there is still a lot of work to do at the top. I recently heard a talk at a meeting of senior HR professionals. The speaker was highlighting how successful a major bank was in hiring migrant workers as cleaners for its offices in London and was lauding this as best practice. These people had the right to work here. Is this really best practice?

Who's an immigrant anyway?

Essentially it comes down to the belief that there is such a thing as a foreigner in England and that immigrants cost the 'native' people in England money and jobs and bring social disharmony. Nobody who reads the daily newspapers can be left without the impression that all immigrants are benefit cheats and scroungers of the state. Yet nothing could be further from the truth.

The truth is probably that we are all immigrants and the vast majority of us contribute heavily to society. Yes, you . . . whether you are white, drink tea at the Savoy and listen to Radio 4 in the morning, whether you are Pakistani and work as an investment banker in the city, or whether you are Turkish and run your own company, you make a huge difference – as an immigrant or the likely descendant of an immigrant.

From the Celts who came from outside Europe in the 7th century, to the Danes, Norse, Norman-French, the German Saxons, and then the Jewish, African Caribbean, Irish, Polish and Asian and Commonwealth immigrants, it is very likely that everyone who lives in Britain today is either an immigrant or the descendant of an immigrant. Everyone could probably trace immigration in their family history if they went back far enough. If we therefore all went 'home to where we came from' it is likely that there would be no one here.

In 2004 the British National Party (BNP) won 11 seats in the UK and it is Britain's fastest growing political party. They campaign for 'native Britons' and for a country where those from other nationalities are welcome to 'go home', even if they are third-generation Britons and are perfectly entitled to live here. So where do they draw the line on what it is to be native? Judging by the BNP website, in their manifesto they seem to accept everyone from mainland Europe who came here. Everyone who just happens to be a white immigrant. Immigrant all the same.

> *'The British National Party exists to secure a future for the indigenous peoples of these islands in the North Atlantic which have been our homeland for millennia. We use the term indigenous to describe the people whose ancestors were the earliest settlers here after the last great Ice Age and which have been complemented by the historic migrations from mainland Europe. The migrations of the Celts, Anglo-Saxons, Danes, Norse and closely related kindred peoples have been, over the past few thousand years, instrumental in defining the character of our family of nations.'*

Clearly those from 'mainland Europe' are included in the Family of Nations. Migrants from non-white countries are not, even though all of these groups are immigrants. Not all are welcomed as family it seems!

So why did people from outside of the North Atlantic come here? Are they all greedy economic migrants as the BNP and mass media might have us believe? Are we being swamped?

The real story of immigration

In the book *Roots of the Future,* Mayerlene Frow examines the contribution of immigration to Britain and highlights that people came to Britain for many diverse reasons: 'In some cases peaceably, as settlers, others were hostile invaders. Thousands arrived as refugees from wars, famines, or civil or religious persecution in their own countries.' After the world wars immigrants were essential to the rebuilding of Britain, to keep the manufacturing industry alive and to start the NHS, which would have failed as soon as it was born without immigrant labour being sought actively from overseas.

Frow goes on to say: 'Some were invited by the monarch or the government to settle here because they had particular skills that were in short supply in Britain. Some were brought against their will as slaves or servants.' That doesn't sound like a one-way relationship to me.

Let's assume that most people in Britain came here legally. So, are we still being swamped? The clear answer is 'no'. Immigrants from minority ethnic communities account for less than 9% of the population. The majority of immigrants are white (61%) and also British-born. Because newcomers have often settled in certain cities, with cheap housing and near members of their own community to provide support, this has led to local people imagining that they are taking over the country. The largest proportion of minority ethnic people tend to live in the cities; outside of the cities, which is the majority of the country, numbers are insignificant. It is also interesting that the number of people who emigrate from the UK each year to make their home in other countries is greater than the number who immigrate here.

Regarding the immigrants who have settled here, it is worth noting, as Frow argues: 'Even a cursory examination would show that immigrants are among the more productive citizens. Some have brought skills and qualifications that are in short supply; others have set up businesses and created work, not only for themselves and also local people; and many of them have been able to do jobs that employers have found difficulty in filling locally.'

She goes on to say: 'Immigrants with the fresh perspective they bring as outsiders are often a catalyst for change. Far from impoverishing the nation as some still claim, immigrants have brought enormous benefit to Britain.'

Not everything is black and white

There is no single factor that is preventing those from BME populations from succeeding and fulfilling their potential. Key factors include poverty and deprivation, but these affect all communities, including those from white working-class backgrounds. Even so it is worth remembering that minority communities are likely to live in some of the most deprived areas of Britain.

In addition to being from a minority community, there is often the burden of discrimination based on skin colour. It is complex. Frow comments that not all immigrants are considered 'problems' by communities, 'just the ones who appear 'different', because of their race or colour, or the way they dress, or the fact they speak another language other than English'. She remarks: 'With almost no primary immigration from the New Commonwealth countries in recent years, the persistence of such claims inevitably suggests that second or third generation of British-born, non-white ethnic minorities are regarded as undesirable immigrants.'

Consider the fact that the UK has one of the fastest growing numbers of mixed inter-racial marriages in the world. Not everything is black and white. Often children from mixed marriages are cast into certain racial categories and it was only in the 2001 census in the UK that a category of 'mixed' was recognised.

Other reasons for discrimination highlighted include peer pressure, overt racism and institutional racism, the latter recognised in the wake of the murder of Stephen Lawrence and the self-reflection of the Metropolitan Police Service (MPS). The MPS now is arguably one of the leading organisations driving diversity forward in the UK.

Low teacher expectation is also a key factor, together with stereotyping that students from black communities are more aggressive, thus justifying harsher treatment.

Each of these elements could fill books in themselves and I have listed in the Resources section where you can go to read more. This book does not claim to be and was not intended to be a comprehensive study of discrimination, immigration or racism. Our only purpose here was to show you that there is a need for a book looking at issues for the BME community, which we hope we have done.

Resources

This resource list was compiled from several magazines, bibliographies in books and websites focusing on BME issues. It is not exhaustive and I have compiled information only as it was presented. The authors take no credit for this compilation. There might be many organisations that are not listed but can provide a good service. None of the websites' content is the responsibility of the authors.

The National Mentoring Network (NMN)

The National Mentoring Network collaborates with over 1,600 organisations and exists to help support the growth of mentoring in its various forms. Its aims are to:

- promote the development of mentoring
- offer advice and support to those wishing to set up or develop mentoring programmes
- provide a forum for the exchange of information and good practice.

Contact them at:

First Floor Charles House
Albert Street
Eccles
M30 0PW

Tel: 0161 787 8600
Fax: 0161 787 8100

Website: www.nmn.org.uk

The National Mentoring Consortium (NMC)

The NMC is a nationally recognised organisation that provides the expertise, training and employer contacts for its mentoring schemes. It works with over 300 employers and 16 universities in the UK.

It has run schemes at every level of the education system as well as for the unemployed and young offenders. It is endorsed by the Institute of Directors, the Institute of Personal Development and the Commission for Racial Equality, among others.

The NMC's main aims are to support disadvantaged and ethnic minority communities around the country and provide quality services and management development programmes. One of its main programmes targets undergraduates.

The scheme is a process whereby ethnic minority undergraduates are linked with mentors – professionals from the world of work – in order to gain support and experience. It is a one-to-one relationship where students can improve their personal and professional skills and prepare for entry into the world of work.

The scheme lasts for six months, from October/November through to April. Monthly mentor and student meetings are held either at the mentor's workplace or at another convenient location. Training and introduction events precede the start of the scheme in October/November.

Contact at University of East London:

Tel: 020 8223 4343

Fax: 020 8223 4986

Email: nmc-online@uel.ac.uk

Windsor Fellowship

This leading national charity runs several programmes for students at all school levels from primary to undergraduate, enabling them to benefit from mentoring, work placements with the UK's leading organisations, and academic and personal support to achieve their aspirations.

The AIMS programme works in-house with schools to provide a ten-week course to the whole class regardless of ethnicity but especially focused on meeting the needs of children at risk of exclusion or underperformance.

The Junior Fellowship programme works with students from 14 to 16 years old who are 'gifted and talented', helping them to maximise their learning. The Leadership Programme for Undergraduates works with high-potential undergraduates, helping to provide seminars and a work placement in a sponsoring company with the aim of encouraging them to prepare for senior roles in organisations. Organisations involved include the Home Office, the BBC, the Bank of England and the South East NHS Strategic Health Authority.

For a detailed overview of all the Fellowship's programmes contact:

Tel: 020 7613 0373

Fax: 020 7613 0377

Email: Info@Windsor-fellowship.org

Website: www.windsor-fellowship.org

Sponsors for Educational Opportunity (SEO)

This organisation, which was founded in New York in 1963, provides internships and development workshops with the UK's leading investment banks.

The programme, open to undergraduate BME students considering a career in investment banking, is supported by Merrill Lynch, Goldman Sachs, Deutsche Bank among many other leading firms.

To contact them:

SEO London
78 Fleet Street
London EC4Y 1HY
Tel: 0845 450 7830
Fax: 0845 450 7831
Email: info@seo-london.org

Website: www.seo-london.org

Civil Service, Ethnic Minority Summer Development Programme

The Summer Development Programme has been running since 1999. Trainees are offered 6–8-week full-time placements in various government departments to gain a more thorough understanding of the type of work Fast Streamers do in the Civil Service.

Wherever trainees are placed they will benefit from core training activities. As part of the programme trainees are invited to attend a three-day residential training course. Working individually as well as in groups, trainees attend workshops and exercises that enhance their understanding of the Civil Service.

Here they learn skills that will stand them in good stead for any career, including leadership, teamwork, time management, presentation and organisational skills.

By the end of the course trainees will have discovered a great deal about the role of the Civil Service and about the relationships between Parliament and Civil Service departments. With a real understanding of Civil Service work and training behind them, the intention is that trainees feel confident enough to apply to the Fast Stream.

For more information please contact:

Cabinet Office
67 Tufton Street
London SW1P 3QS

Website: http://xenergy.diversity.faststream.gov.uk

Global Graduates

This organisation, set up in 1999, provides a range of services to help BME students consider a career in law. Through the Diversity in Law programme they look to improve students' knowledge and awareness about the law sector and, most crucially, build on the essential skills demanded of any trainee solicitor, such as writing and presentation/interview techniques. In addition to the seminars and workshops that run during the academic year disseminating such information, students have the invaluable opportunity to arrange appointments to receive one-to-one advice and reviews of CVs, application forms and interview techniques.

Contact:

Global Graduates
15–17 Ridgmount Street,

London WC1E 7AH
Tel: 020 7291 1375
Fax: 020 7291 1249
Email: yo@diversityinlaw.com

National Black Boys Can Association

This is a national programme whose aim is to raise the social and academic aspirations of Black boys between the ages of 9 and 16. The main offering is the Black Boys Can training and development programme which:

- aims to build black boys' self-confidence and motivate them to educational and social success
- assists them in developing strategies for dealing with adverse factors that often impede their progress
- operates within a positive environment where boys learn to value themselves and others
- is taught by positive role models, people who believe in the ability of black boys to succeed.

This extra support is given to supplement what they are already being taught at school and is not designed to replace the important role that their school teachers play in their education.

Most projects operate on Saturday mornings on a fortnightly basis. There is also a franchise programme that can be purchased and is supported by the organisation.

Contact:

Email: blackboyscan@hotmail.com

Website: www.blackboyscan.co.uk

100 Black Men of London

This organisation consists of a group of concerned African-Caribbean men. The 100 Black Men of London seek to improve the quality of life in our communities and to enhance educational and economic opportunities through pooling collective resources.

More than 10,000 dedicated mentors and volunteer members have touched the lives of over 120,000 youths. Through programmes that place a heavy emphasis on mentoring, education, health and well-being and economic development, youth are empowered to reach their full potential. The first international chapter of 100 Black Men was formed in Birmingham (UK) in December 1997. The London chapter was formed in 2001.

For more information see:

www.100bmol.org.uk

Race for Opportunity (RFO), MERLIN and the London Accord

These Business in the Community-related organisations provide a wide range of services to employers and resources and support to schools to encourage the achievement of BME students and employees.

MERLIN provides a resource pack to teachers and offers an excellent video containing lessons that can be used in the National Curriculum featuring BME role models. RFO can provide mentoring contacts to engage employers with schools and the community as well as to improve access to BME applicants.

Contact:

Race for Opportunity
137 Shepherdess Walk
London N1 7RQ
Tel: 020 7566 8087
Fax: 020 7253 1877
MERLIN
London Accord
137 Shepherdess Walk
London N1 7RQ
Tel: 020 7566 8656
Email: London-accord@bitc.org.uk

Website: www.londonaccord.org.uk

Advice can also be sought from the following organisations:

Commission for Racial Equality

St Dunstan's House
201–211 Borough High Street
London SE1 1GZ
Tel: 020 7939 0000
Fax: 020 7939 0001
Email: info@cre.gov.uk

Website: www.cre.gov.uk

The Commission for Racial Equality is the government body for monitoring and advising on race issues in Britain. The website covers areas such as law, publications and a self-help guide.

Institute for Race Relations

2–6 Leeke Street
London WC1X 9HS
Tel: 0207 833 210 or 0207 837 0041

The Refugee Council

3–9 Bondway
London SW8 1SJ
Tel: 0207 582 6922

Can supply a free resource list and put you in touch with potential speakers.

The Runnymede Trust

London Fruit & Wool Exchange
Brushfield Street
London E1 6EP
Tel: 0207 377 6622 or 0207 377 9222

Website: www.runnymedetrust.org

Advice and resources on race and policy issues. They also produce a very informative monthly bulletin for educationalists.

Magazines

Below are some magazines that focus on careers, in particular for BME students.

Smaart Talent, published by Smaart Publishing, Quarterly

This magazine is published in association with the Windsor Fellowship and is aimed at BME students. It is available as an e-magazine at www.windsor-fellowship.org

Black History Month, published by Sugar Media, annually

Tel: 020 740 77747

Futures, a career magazine for BME students, also published by Sugar Media

Tel: 020 740 77747

Books

Here are some resources for teachers which can be used in the classroom and to better understand the issues affecting BME pupils.

The main source for specialist books on these subjects is Trentham Books. It has a full catalogue available on the web and is highly recommended.

Trentham Books

Westview House

734 London Road

Oakhill

Stoke-on-Trent ST4 5NP

Tel: 01782 745 567

Publishes 'Multicultural Teaching' magazine and a wide range of multicultural/anti-racist books.

Toolkit for Tackling Racism in Schools

A resource pack full of practical ideas for staff development and curriculum planning.

Stella Dadzie, Trentham Books, 2000, £12.99. ISBN: 1 858 56188 4

Roots of the Future: Ethnic Diversity in the Making of Britain

Crammed with information about the huge contribution made by ethnic minorities to Britain's economic, political, social and cultural development.

Commission for Racial Equality, 1996, £9.95. ISBN: 1 854 42179 4

Still No Problem Here: Anti-Racism in Predominantly White Schools

Informative discussion of the issues, with practical suggestions for schools.

Chris Gaine, Trentham Books, 1995, £14.99. ISBN: 1 858 56013 6

Gender, 'Race' and Class in Schooling: A New Introduction

An accessible background information and research summary.

Chris Gaine and Rosalyn George, RoutledgeFalmer, 1998, £23.99. ISBN: 0 750 70757 7

Equality Assurance in Schools: A Handbook for Action Planning and School Effectiveness

A useful schools' guide with practical advice on planning and implementing broad equality plans with a focus on race issues and a good bibliography on equality issues across the curriculum. A booklet of INSET activities is also available.

Trentham Books and The Runnymede Trust, 1994, £8.95. ISBN: 0 948 08091 4

Spanner in the Works: Education for Racial Equality and Social Justice in White Schools

Clare Brown, Jacqui Barnfield and Mary Stone, Trentham Books, 1990, £10.99. ISBN: 0 948 08038 8

Anti-Racist Curriculum Guidelines

A useful teachers' handbook.

National Union of Teachers, revised version 2001, *www.teachers.org.uk*

Challenging racism – Racism: resources for use

National Youth Agency, 1989, 17–23 Albion Street, Leicester, LE1 6GD

Additional teacher resources

Show Racism the Red Card

A video, CD-ROM with various study notes and worksheets.

SRTRC, 1 Drury Lane, Newcastle upon Tyne, NE1 1EA, £15

All Different, All Equal

Very useful classroom and teachers' resource pack, with a video, for practical anti-racist and multicultural teaching in schools. For KS 3/4. Photocopied materials can be bought from NEAD at £5.

COMPASS, Norfolk Education & Action for Development, 38 Exchange Street, Norwich NR2 1AX. Tel: 01603 610 993

Equaliser II

Activities and ideas for empowerment and anti-racist work with young people.

Bread Youth Project, 1996, £13. ISBN: 0 951 83571 8

Anti-Racist Education Pack

Activities and information, designed by young people for young people.

Youth Against Racism in Europe, 1995, £2.50

Off Limits: Talking About Race

Three stimulating 20-minute videos in which a group of young people discuss identity, racism, multiculturalism and how teachers should deal with these issues.

Channel 4 Schools, PO Box 100, Warwick, CV34 6TZ. 1997. Video £9.95; teachers' guide £4.95

Let's Talk About Racism

A KS3 children's book.

Angela Grunsell, Franklin Watts, 1990, £8.99. ISBN: 0 749 60432 8

How Racism Came to Britain: A Cartoon History

Institute of Race Relations, 1985, £3.50. ISBN: 0 850 01029 2

Websites

Below are some websites that you might find interesting.

www.100greatblackbritons.com

A useful site with biographies of Black Britons, with links and ideas for schools.

www.channel4.com/origination

A website with interesting resources for individuals and schools related to diversity.

www.blackpresence.co.uk

An excellent website focusing on all aspects of British black history.

www.irespect.net

Aimed at schools and education practitioners. Promoting positive tolerance.

www.antiracist.org.uk

Includes anti-racist teaching materials.

www.carf.demon.co.uk

'CARF' (Campaign Against Racism & Fascism) is an independent anti-racist magazine, chronicling British and European resistance to racism. It is also a resource and information base for community-based campaigns, co-ordinating and servicing many grassroots anti-racist initiatives.

www.homebeats.co.uk

Homebeats highlights the Homebeats CD-ROM produced by the Institute of Race Relations, which is about the history of race relations in Britain and relationships with other parts of the world. The site gives updates on news and events concerning the CD-ROM.

http://news.bbc.co.uk/1/hi/uk/1993597.stm

Lots of links to UK-based information.

www.search.eb.com/Blackhistory/home/do

Encyclopaedia Britannica on black history.

www.oxfam.org.uk/coolplanet

A handy site for pupils and educators involved in global education issues. Presented in age categories.

www.britkid.org

A fantastic interactive website with resources for students and teachers. Highly recommended.

www.letterboxlibrary.com

A collection of children's books that celebrate equality and diversity.

www.multikulti.org.uk

Provides information, advice, guidance and learning materials in community languages.

www.obv.org.uk

A resource centre for practical ways to engage BME people to be active citizens in political representation and decision making.

Business mentoring organisations

The Prince's Trust

www.Princes-trust.org.uk

Mentoring and business support for 16–30-year-olds.

Shell Live Wire

www.shell-livewire.org/

Similar to the Prince's Trust with awards for entrepreneurs.

Publisher's acknowledgements

We are grateful to the following for permission to reproduce copyright material:

Photograph of windsurfers on Negril beach, Jamaica ©mediacolor's/Alamy; Colin Salmon photograph ©Rune Hellestad/Corbis; Saundra Glenn photograph with thanks to the European Federation of Black Women Business Owners; Sir Bill Morris photograph ©EMPICS/PA; Asif Kisson photograph with thanks to Jab Promotions; Janet Soo-Chung photograph with thanks to David Hague and Mohan Ahad photograph with thanks to the Centre for Entrepreneurial Learning, University of Cambridge.

In some instances we have been unable to trace the owners of copyright material, and we would appreciate any information that would enable us to do so.

Authors' acknowledgements

Steven:

I would like to thank my parents Silo and Christine, my brother Selwyn and my sister Charlene for being unfailing role models of unconditional love – even when I don't deserve it. Also my uncle Theo who taught me implicitly that I can write a book – only because he wrote several!

I would also like to thank Omar Ismail, who has demonstrated to me what really taking a stand for others is about, and who is my own role model for friendship, leadership and integrity. I would like to thank all my friends and colleagues, past and present, who have helped support me in actually completing a project for once – you know who you are! – it would take another book to name you all personally). It was only your constant support and encouragement that helped this book happen. Thank you to Eda, my partner, for being my rock, someone that accepts me and sustains me. To Elena for being my writing and personal coach, lending me titles that I forget to return! And Katie Napier, web manager extraordinaire.

Thank you to Jagroop Kaur-Dhillon (OLMEC) and Sandra Kerr, from Race for Opportunity, your enthusiasm and support gave me the 'second wind' to believe in the project and for opening your connections to me. Patrick for being not only my co-author, but my inspiration, telling me to 'aim higher'. Thank you also to Maqsood Ahmad, Kevin Coutinho, Urooj Amjad, Kishor Mistry, Beverley Stewart, Ian Chivers and Sue Henely for your support. Inge Fisher especially for telling me I could not start anything new before finishing this project.

I would like to acknowledge Jonathan Robinson, one of the co-founders of the Hub, for introducing me to Rachael Stock, my fantastic publisher, and Laura for doing such a painstaking editing job. Thank you especially to Bola Ogun, Windsor

Fellowship staff and trustees, and the Home Office who was my sponsor, for giving me the opportunity to 'learn to lead' and to all the organisations who have sponsored copies of this book to give free to schools, colleges, universities and networks so we can inspire our younger generation. Lastly I would like to thank each of the role models in this book for sparing their time to share their stories, and you the reader, for taking the time to listen to them.

Patrick:

I have three young boys, Conrad 10, Alexander 6 and Theodore 5 – I know that both my wife Sonji and I are truly their role models.

I must thank Paul Cuttill, Chief Operating Officer at EDF Energy, for not only supporting this important book, but also for being a true role model to many.

My uncle 'Arry', what can I say to you but thank you, you are my biggest role model.

About the authors

Steven D'Souza is a leading organisational diversity specialist, consultant, speaker, writer and personal and career development coach; focusing on inspiring possibilities and creating results for diverse individuals, groups and organisations.

He has held consultant and management roles in high performing companies such as Merrill Lynch Europe Plc, Abbey Plc, Radisson Edwardian Ltd and while at the Windsor Fellowship coached students in strategies for success on behalf of various major public and private sector organisations including the Home Office, the BBC, Goldman Sachs and the Foreign Office. He has worked as an Assessor for the Home Office Network and the Probation Service Network and has written for various diversity and educational publications such as *The Independent's* 'Opportunity' magazine, Smaart Talent, and also *Hobsons Career Guides* for Minority Ethnic Students. Steven sits on the Governing Board of the City of Westminster College, London, and is committed to supporting educational attainment, business partnerships and community engagement.

To personally contact Steven and for more information and inspirational resources please visit his website, *www.possibilityplanet.co.uk*

Born on the 4th of July in Jamaica, **Patrick Clarke** is an experienced general manager, initially trained in Electrical Engineering and now trying to develop an interim career in Human Resources and Communications. He describes himself as specialising in people and has spent much of the last 25 years 'giving back' to his communities.

As well as the numerous senior roles held by Patrick within EDF Energy and other companies, Patrick is particularly proud of his many community responsibilities during the past 25 years. He became a school governor a few years after leaving school in the early 80's, joined the then Police 'Force' not service as a result of the 1984 Brixton riots. Immediately after leaving the police he became one of the early Lay Visitors to police stations in Lambeth and eventually vice-chair of this body. He went on to further engage with his community by taking on a trustee's role within a small housing association responsible for a stock of 400 houses.

Over this period Patrick specialised in spending time in local schools imparting his learning and experience to young children. He is currently Chairman and Director of a social enterprise and charity responsible for the running of a children's breakfast club, children's day nursery, after school club, community care and a canteen.

To personally contact Patrick please email him at Patrickclarke@hotmail.co.uk